PRAISE FOR ADRIAN KULP
AND *DAD OR ALIVE*

"If this is what 'staying at home' is like, then please throw me to the razor-wolves of outside reality any day."
—Patton Oswalt, author of *Zombie Spaceship Wasteland*

"If I've learned anything from this book, it's to keep your weight on your back foot while interacting with a child. It makes for a swifter escape."
—Kevin Nealon, author of *Yes, You're Pregnant, but What About Me?*

"As a new father myself, this book is essential. I've learned immensely from Adrian and become a better parent by learning from his countless mistakes. This book is proof that he's let down his children time after time and also highlights the unreliability of Child Protective Services."
—Steve Byrne, cocreator/writer/producer/star of *Sullivan & Son*

"This book made me laugh. So much fresher and funnier than the diapers he's been changing—you're in for a great read!"
—Louie Anderson, author of *The F Word: How to Survive Your Family*

"Adrian and I have known each other a long time. We used to hang out a lot more. Then he had a family and became an amazing dad. And I felt bad for him. Not because of the father thing but because he's an Eagles fan."   —Nick Swardson, comedian

"Adrian Kulp shines a per⬛⬛⬛⬛⬛⬛⬛⬛⬛⬛⬛⬛⬛tay-at-home dad and fatherho⬛⬛⬛⬛⬛⬛⬛⬛⬛⬛⬛orm. I love a man in a Björn."⬛⬛⬛⬛⬛⬛⬛⬛⬛⬛⬛⬛edian

"Not only is this book h⬛⬛⬛⬛⬛⬛⬛⬛⬛⬛⬛⬛ every-thing Adrian is talking ab⬛⬛⬛⬛⬛⬛is a must-have. Now, go and buy it."   —Jo Koy, comedian

perfect hilarious light on being a spe...
...tood in general. Forget a man in unif...
—Wendy Liebman, com...

...hysterical, but I can also relate to...
...bout Dad or Mom...

DAD OR ALIVE

CONFESSIONS OF AN
UNEXPECTED STAY-AT-HOME DAD

ADRIAN KULP

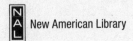 New American Library

New American Library
Published by the Penguin Group
Penguin Group (USA) Inc., 375 Hudson Street,
New York, New York 10014, USA

USA / Canada / UK / Ireland / Australia
New Zealand / India / South Africa / China

Penguin Books Ltd., Registered Offices: 80 Strand, London WC2R 0RL,
England
For more information about the Penguin Group visit penguin.com.

First published by New American Library,
a division of Penguin Group (USA) Inc.

First Printing, May 2013

 REGISTERED TRADEMARK—MARCA REGISTRADA

LIBRARY OF CONGRESS CATALOGING-IN-PUBLICATION DATA:
Kulp, Adrian.
Dad or alive: confessions of an unexpected stay-at-home dad/Adrian Kulp.
p. cm.
ISBN 978-0-451-41333-8
1. Fathers—Humor. 2. Fatherhood—Humor. 3. Parenting—Humor. I. Title.
PN6231.F37K85 2013
306.874'20207—dc23   2012046910

Printed in the United States of America
10 9 8 7 6 5 4 3 2 1

Set in Jansen Text
Designed by Spring Hoteling

PUBLISHER'S NOTE
Penguin is committed to publishing works of quality and integrity. In that
spirit, we are proud to offer this book to our readers; however the story, the
experiences and the words are the author's alone.

While the author has made every effort to provide accurate telephone numbers, Internet addresses, and other contact information at the time of publication, neither the publisher nor the author assumes any responsibility for errors,
or for changes that occur after publication. Further, publisher does not have
any control over and does not assume any responsibility for author or third-
party Web sites or their content.

For Jen, an amazing wife, best friend and mom. Without you none of this would've been possible, I love you.

CONTENTS

CHAPTER TEN

CHAPTER ELEVEN

ACKNOWLEDGMENTS

DAD OR ALIVE

CHAPTER 1

Forget About the Game, We've Got Shit to Do

GAME FIVE

I've been a die-hard baseball fan for as long as I can remember. My dad and I used to play catch every day during the summer when he got home from work. On the rare occasion he knew he was going to be late, he tacked a piece of carpet up against the brick on the side of the house so I could practice my aim.

He's a mason by trade, and I think he was always proud that we could use his brick handiwork as the backdrop to support me in honing my skills. Once he was home, he'd hit me pop-ups and grounders, complete with ad-libbed broadcast commentary and constructive criticism.

"You've gotta hustle on those, Adrian. While you were busy putting on your lipstick and mascara, the runner just took two instead of holding him to a single," he said.

I practiced every day and continued to play for a number

of years. I started as an outfielder, and because I was left-handed, I later moved on to play first base. There was nothing better than the smell of the freshly cut grass and perfectly groomed infield. I loved baseball.

I was from Philadelphia and the Phillies were always my guys. My family lived and breathed the home team, and from an early age, they had me outfitted with a healthy stock of swag. Being any type of Philly sports fan took stamina and patience. The modern World Series was created in 1903, and it took us seventy-seven years to win our first ring—in 1980. It was the powerhouse team of Michael Jack Schmidt, Pete Rose, and Steve Carlton that had us gathered around the TV set every summer night. I could never pronounce our third baseman's nickname and my family got a kick out of me jumping around the living room yelling, "C'mon, shitty!"

I was only four years old at the time, but like a devoted little slugger, I already had plenty of memorabilia. I wore Phillies footie pajamas in the winter and had pennants from Veterans Stadium on the wall of my bedroom. I can almost remember sitting in the living room watching the game with my dad and uncles, systematically cruising around the coffee table, stealing the backwash from the bottom of their Heinekens, and clapping along with them. It was male bonding at its best.

Fast forward twenty-nine years.

I still have those old stained pennants that hung in my room the year they won it all. The love affair and the subsequent collection has grown. I have a half dozen jerseys in my closet, bobbleheads and collector pins. I've got empty Phils soda cans, Tastykake promo wrappers, *Philly Inquirers*, autographed balls and rookie cards on the shelf. Don't ask me why, but I even kept an empty Phils' Kleenex box.

Next to my nightstand, on the wall, hang pictures of me playing baseball as a kid, as well as a picture of me on TV in 2008 (the year the Phillies won their second World Series). I was sitting in the stands directly behind home plate during a night game in Los Angeles. With the cameras fixed on me, announcers Tom McCarthy and Chris Wheeler commented on and pondered how a Phillies fan had managed to get a seat behind home plate in Dodger Stadium. They zoomed in on me as I screamed to root on our shortstop Jimmy Rollins with an invasive and boisterous holler that carried into the loge and beyond. I didn't care about the gangbangers behind me threatening to "open me up" in the parking lot. I was concerned only that Jimmy heard me and it would somehow give him the inspiration to clear the bases.

A lot had changed over the years. I was now thirty-three years old. It could be said that I shared a lot of ups and downs with my favorite team, small achievements but no huge wins. Things lost, friends come and gone, but baseball was always a constant. I was there for her and she was there for me.

It was October. Any baseball fan knows what October means. Playoff baseball. The best kind of baseball there is. There was electricity in the air that could make the hair on your arms stand up. My team had taken out the Colorado Rockies to win the NLDS. Three days later, they moved on to face the Dodgers in the NLCS. It was a split series with each team taking two wins. It came down to a final game five to decide who would go to the World Series. The Phils could go for the second year in a row and potentially win for only the third time in their history.

It was hard, knowing that this was all happening a few miles away on the other end of the 10 Freeway. I wasn't there, because the timing of my wife's pregnancy made it too risky to go. Jen was nine months along, and the very last thing I needed was to have her water break while I was cracking peanuts and bottoming out beers with a painted face along the first-base line.

I had come home from work early that day and commandeered the living room. I donned my favorite ball cap and Chase Utley jersey and collected my good luck charms: a foul ball I still hold on to today during tenuous situations (as a child, it landed in my seat during a trip to the bathroom and the guy next to me returned it along with the story when I came back) and rally towel, FedExed to me by my mom. The son of a woman she worked with was at Citizens Bank Park a few nights before as they gave them out. It made it all the way from the bleachers to my living room, and it was legit.

I scrubbed the sour stink off of my zip-up beer Koozie and even gave the flat screen a quick buff. Snacks were prepared, my phone was on vibrate, and I had gone ahead and deleted any TV show reminders that might pop up on my DVR, trying to interrupt and record over the history that was about to be made. It looked as if I had opened up a Dick's Sporting Goods store in the living room.

This was going to be it. I could feel it in my bones. Could they go all the way for only the second time that I could remember? I stood up, hat over my heart in my living room, singing along to the national anthem, and watched the first pitch come out. I sat down and surrendered myself to the leather sofa for the next three hours.

And that's when I heard Jen from the other room—

"Adrian, can you come in here?" she asked.

I pretended not to hear her, but it came around a second time.

"Forget about the game, we've got shit to do."

She said it nonchalantly, as if she hadn't noticed the "Occupy: Game Five" movement I had established in the other room.

It felt as if a bag of gas-soaked charcoal briquettes had just ignited inside my head. I was short of breath and closing in on convulsions. I caught a waft of the fabled burnt toast you smell before you kick over from an aneurysm. Reality was pounding at my front door. It had brought Chuck Norris along, and together they were warming up their legs to drop a roundhouse spin kick to the face of my special night. I had put "this" off until the eleventh hour.

"This" was the nursery.

The guest bedroom of our two-bedroom apartment in Playa del Rey, California, had a split personality. Sometimes it functioned as a place for visitors to sleep, but more than often, it was my default man cave. It was our home office and the future nursery for our first child, a girl. Other than letting her live in one of our cars or the mailbox, it was the logical choice and the only option as to where we would house this baby.

We weren't even close to having it squared away. And when my wife gets something that she wants to do in her head, there's really no arguing. The guest bedroom (man cave) was being laid to rest, and I was to be the one who would dig the hole and throw the first shovel of dirt.

Historically, I'm a procrastinator, and I'd put this off for weeks and now months. Maybe there was a part of me that was holding off as long as possible. Maybe if I didn't see a nursery, it meant we weren't having a kid. I was having trouble coming to grips with the idea of having to dismantle and box everything up.

Up until this point, I led a fairly self-centered existence and was consumed with my hobbies and interests. In my twenties my possessions, collectibles, and memorabilia had defined me. To box them up and cast them into the darkness of a storage unit was a tough pill to swallow.

But this was a big moment in my life. It was time to evolve, time to stop being so selfish and finally grow up. It was incredibly tough to part with a bunch of crap that only I considered valuable, but the reality was that it wasn't going to the incinerator, just being put in the corner on a time-out to be enjoyed later.

I really tried to cut the cord and go cold turkey. I made excuses to myself and my wife as to why some things had to stay. What if there was a fire at the storage facility? What if we somehow forgot to pay the bill and I saw the guys on *Storage Wars* fighting over my shit on primetime cable? Then what?

I begrudgingly turned up the volume on the TV and moved to the other room to face my fears. I slowly started removing the least-important toys from their positions. Like some sort of junkie, I started shoving and hiding my faves in the cabinets, under the bed, and above the refrigerator, thinking that if the TEA (Toy Enforcement Agency) came, they wouldn't find my stash.

What I really needed was to rip the Band-Aid off. The slow peel was just too painful.

My worlds were colliding on the battlefield that was the guest bedroom. Jen picked up on my erratic behavior and confronted me with an intervention in the middle of the hall-way, where I was busy burying figurines in the closet behind the linens.

"Adrian, what's going on with you? Are you being serious right now? You're a grown man hiding G.I. Joes in between pillowcases. It's time, hon. It's time to grow up," she said.

Becoming a dad was an unfamiliar experience and was evidently coming with a giant learning curve. If I'd picked up on anything from the men in my life—uncles, married peers, and Al Bundy—it was "don't mess with pregnant women." Lucky for me, at this particular moment, that nugget of wisdom was echoing through the halls of my vacuous head.

I was about to put on some big-boy pants. I was committing a selfless act. It wasn't just about me anymore. Sure, it was painful missing this game and giving up my toys. I know a lot of people reading this are probably thinking that I should just suck it up and stop being a pussy, but I suppose it's easier said than done for some of us. Maybe I was just a late bloomer. Hell, I grew another four inches during my senior year in high school. And to this day, I still can't grow a full beard. I had trouble making the transition. Surely I couldn't be the only one.

So what did she want to do in here? Was I just supposed to put a decent dent in this or what? Was it something that I could knock out in three innings and get back to the arm-chair while my pretzel bites were still warm, or was I here for the long haul?

"Let's take everything off the walls and get this bed and box spring out of here," she said.

I don't know if you're familiar with the work-distribution model while working with a pregnant woman, but it's basically a one-man job. I pulled the pillows from the bed, a dozen of them lined up like a cemetery of headstones, each with their own decorative sham. I Frisbeed them along to Jen, who was armed with garbage bags, ready to tape up and label.

I took apart the bed frame and got emotionally and physically prepared for the main event: wrestling our queen-sized mattress and box spring through two doorways, out of this tiny bedroom, and into the living room.

I stood the beast up vertically. I twisted and turned the mattress, then my lower back. Several attempts later, I had it hung up on the wall and wedged under one of the doorjambs as my wife offered words of encouragement from the other side of the fracas, which quickly turned to yelling as I knocked framed pictures of our grandparents off the wall. I had this thing stuck, now partially between two doorways, and was exerting great effort to make the turn. Clearly, my future as a furniture mover was not in the cards. To make matters worse, something big was happening with the game in the other room. The crowd noise was peaking, and I couldn't get out there to check on it.

I could hear a voice faintly ask if I wanted any help. Ha. Sure . . . help. I yelled through the mattress and refused because it was obvious that I didn't need help. What's next? Am I going to stop and ask for directions next time I'm lost? Doubtful. It was also clear that she was physically unable to help me, which was probably half of the reason she offered.

I reached the point of complete frustration and could hear the announcers and erupting crowd on the other side of the wall yelling about the big play. With the roar of the fans behind me, I inflated my chest and scuffed my hoof on the carpet like a bull preparing to storm the matador. I took off and tackled the pillow-top Serta. My Phillies hat, now completely drenched in sweat, was knocked askew as I muscled the beast through the doorway, spinning off of it and spilling onto the living room floor in a disheveled heap.

"Can you take it easy for a minute?" my wife said, sitting on the sofa holding the remote, as she had just changed the channel to *The Little Couple*. "Yeah, I'm fine," I said, as I checked my knees for rug burn, picked myself off the floor, and mustered up some composure. "I just wanted to see this play."

"All right, let's get the floor vacuumed and then grab something to stand on," she said. "I need you to hang this new light.

"I bought a cute frosted dome light cover with silver fixtures, because the one that's up there is too cold and clinical," she added.

"While you're doing that, I'll open up all of this pink bedding and the matching curtains. Where is the crib bumper that was sitting here yesterday? You didn't throw it out, did you? Wait, you didn't put the curtain rod up yet? Can you give me a hand hanging up all of these butterfly mirrors before you put the Diaper Genie together?" she rattled.

Oh. My. God. Someone stop the room from spinning, I needed to get off. It was like my ears were being water tortured. I wondered what might be next. If she broke out some old scrapbook journal of magazine cutouts and brochures that she'd been keeping since she was a child, indicating precisely how her first daughter's room would look, I might get sick. Thank the heavens that Pinterest wasn't invented yet or I'd really be up shit creek without a paddle.

I was steered toward a gallon of semigloss and some rollers, leading me to believe that I was about to paint the room. Pink. Specifically, rosebud pink. I proceeded with my process of taping the trim, corners, and windows while laying plastic down on the floor and applied not one, but two coats.

Jen was all over the place, pregnantly forgetful and demanding. Most of the time she was talking to herself, and it was hard to distinguish the difference between schizophrenic rambling and an actual request directed at me. After the painting was done, I just waited for my number to be picked. Again.

It was kind of like those days on the bus in middle school when the bullies in the back seats decided it was time to delegate wedgies. They started chanting your name, and if you stuck your head up above the top of the seat or showed any indication that this was bothering you, it was T minus ten seconds to atomic detonation, otherwise known as "the embarrassing walk home, carrying the waistband from your underwear." You were about to get power-pulled. You could only pray that they couldn't get it over your head and hook it to your chin, with the girl you were crushing on witnessing the entire thing.

Was she going to start chanting my name with another project? I followed the same approach I did in middle school. I kept a low profile, my head down and buried, as I fumbled around inside my toolbox, pretending to sort sockets. I snuck back into the living room to put the game back on and returned like I had my own agenda, hoping to appear busy enough that I didn't have to be integrated into her madness. I abstained from making eye contact and kept a safe distance, trying to avoid being taken out by her stomach, as she carelessly swung it around the room like a wrecking ball, all while comparing swaths of fabric and checking things off of the honey-do list.

She seemed puzzled for a moment while staring back and forth between the walls and the fabric as if she were doing long division.

"Do the pink walls complement all of the pink bedding and curtains?" she asked. "I don't think they do."

I conjured up a dramatic and concerned look while I stood back to observe. I wasn't the fucking guy to ask, especially right now. I was missing game five, for chrissake. And the only time I've ever spent with the color was on Easter, for two hours every year, when I wore the same pink Van Heusen dress shirt my mom had bought for me at a consignment shop. *Plus*, I had just spent two hours painting this room (twice), and I knew there was no way in hell that I was doing it again.

It was irrelevant whether or not, in my heart, I agreed with her about the shades of pink. I chose to use every tool in my kit to convince her that it looked amazing.

From the other room, I heard, "Phillies win! Phillies win!" I had missed the game, but in the end it didn't matter. I realized that I'd done something important that night. Even if it was somewhat forced, I had done something selfless and had embraced our future as a family. I'd sacrificed the man cave and built a room for my unborn daughter.

And just like baseball was there for me all those years, I would be there for her.

I was going to be a dad.

THE AWKWARD SEX REWARD

I assumed because I had made a selfless, precedent-setting sacrifice in turning my dude chamber into an infant's nursery that I had moved mountains and parted the seas. Because of this, I came to the conclusion that I deserved sex.

Sex was interesting (to say the least) as the pregnancy progressed. As a guy, I've heard the (sub)urban legends about how pregnant women are incessantly horny and demand intercourse around the clock. I was hoping to cash in on some of this lore. We hadn't gotten a ton of practice while trying to conceive. Jen had led me to believe that it could take weeks or months to get pregnant, but alas, after our first dinner and a movie, the seed was planted.

Now, with the threat of pregnancy no longer an issue, it was time to make up some ground. Unfortunately, that's not how it went down. All of those salacious rumblings didn't hold water as well as my wife's belly.

In the beginning, sure, we carried on with our occasional sextracurricular activities as if everything were normal, like there were no real anatomical or emotional implications from the pregnancy, but once seven or eight months rolled around, things changed a bit.

The physical evidence of the third trimester couldn't be ignored. Our bed was overtaken by the Snoogle, a pillow python that consumed a good third of the mattress. Jen could no longer maneuver with ease, and it took calculated planning to make a simple trip to the bathroom. We had switched our sleeping sides to give her an unobstructed path to the bathroom.

Certain "adventurous" positions completely disappeared from our repertoire, and falling back on the old missionary standby required me to protect myself. I'm not talking about prophylactics (according to the ob-gyn, she couldn't get pregnant again!). I'm talking about a back brace.

Pregnant women are absolutely beautiful and, generally speaking, sex is almost always a wonderful thing. And at the risk of being slapped by my wife after she reads into this too much, having sex in the latter stages of pregnancy is kind of like moving a refrigerator. Boom. I said it.

There was a lot of awkward squatting and contorting on my end, trying to wrap my arms around the appliance, hanging on to make sure I didn't drop it on my toes or fall off completely. I occasionally peeked around the left and right sides with limited vision, to make sure I wasn't banging the fridge into any corners.

There's also a mental component to all of this: This large bump was concealing my child. And the idea that my child would use the same canal to enter the world that I'd been using for recreation was mentally debilitating.

I refrained from any dirty talk, because up until this point, I'd been reading fairy tales and playing light classical music into my wife's belly to positively influence this dear, innocent unborn baby. Sexually charged expletives and raunchy clichés were only going to confuse this poor child later in life.

Needless to say, the combination of all of these factors resulted in that night being the last time I attempted any sort of lovemaking with my wife. It was getting a little too close to delivery day and things were getting really askew in my head.

Please don't think I wrote this to dissuade any new expectant fathers from having late-term sex. I was just personally touched by these challenges and had to be careful not to hurt my back, because I undoubtedly had more work to do.

YOU NEED A SHOWER

With only a weekend or two left before delivery, we were more or less staying close to home and scrambling to get all of the last-minute things done that we'd put off.

Several months earlier, we had gone through the registration process for gifts that would be given to us at one of our three baby showers.

THREE. Baby. Showers.

Jen's family lived in Atlanta, mine was in Philly and, at the time, we lived in Los Angeles. Hence, three separate showers at the far reaches of the country. The only way this could've been any worse was if it they'd been in Alaska, Maine, and Florida. Or heaven, purgatory, and hell.

Registering for gifts was fun at first, even if they ultimately weren't for me. We designated a weekend to hit up places like Pottery Barn Kids and Babies "R" Us. These stores were brimming with pregnant women toting behind them shells of men who tried to keep up but not get in the way.

We checked in with the registry liaison, were issued our weapons and told where to start the whole ordeal. What was I supposed to get? How many? Do I buy only girl colors or consider neutral so that we might use them again down the line?

As much as I wanted to go ballistic and light up the whole store with this plastic inventory gun, in the back of my mind, I knew there would be consequences. I had to think before I pulled the trigger. We would eventually have to turn in our weapons, as the liaison downloaded our hit list and we were held accountable for our actions. An audit of our product homicides was right around the corner.

I tried to slow my roll and stick close to Jen during this intimidating process because I was worried we'd shoot the same stuff and didn't want to end up spending additional time weeding through doubles and triples of things.

I generally don't fair well in department stores or quite honestly any shopping situation where I have to stand still for more than thirty seconds or wait for someone else to make a decision on something. Once Jen had any type of idea of what she wanted, even if it were merely a suggestion, I gave the immediate all-clear "I think it's great, honey; you should get it if that's what you want."

As much as I tried to hang back with my wife, my inner John Rambo took over and I found myself straying away on my own mission.

"I'm gonna go and check some things out," I said.

"Shoot anything that looks cool," she offered as I walked away.

Bad move, I thought, as I dropped to one knee and pumped a splat mat full of laser beams.

Anything that looked like it might help us, I killed it. I was actually having a decent time for a little while, twisting my way around the end caps, shooting over an expectant mom's shoulder to waste some sippy cups perched high on the shelf above her head.

It all came to a screeching halt, though, as my wife selfishly interrupted my log rolls through the formula section, signaled she was done, and headed toward the front of the store. I had exhausted myself, was dehydrated, and returned to customer service to pound a Gatorade and face the judge.

As it turns out, we were deadly accurate with 351 kills. Her tally consisted of mainly necessities and personal comfort items. Mine ranged from silicone skins to protect our electronics, LEGOs, and bras with the nipple holes cut out. The problem was, and I knew, everything we had registered for would start showing up at our front door sporadically in the months and weeks leading up to the birth.

It was wonderful that we'd decided to have a baby, but I was beginning to feel a tad awkward that we were making everyone else pay for it. And even worse, that I was going to have to find a home for all these "necessities."

Shortly after that weekend, the gifts started arriving early from those guests who were unable to make the showers. Our dining room had become a real-life game of Tetris, a pyramid of cardboard boxes stacked to the ceiling filled with baby products, squished together to complete an unsightly and unsound structure.

Coed baby showers seemed to be trending at the time, but luckily for my guy friends, Jen and I didn't go that route.

I spared them the torture of missing an NFL Sunday, being huddled around the punch bowl like at a junior high dance. Forced to break out their Sunday "wrinkle-free" Dockers and dress shoes while the girls hoarded cucumber finger sandwiches, talked about exfoliators, *The Bachelorette*, and how much more we could probably do around the house.

The upside of having a traditional women's-only baby shower was that I wasn't required to show up until the very end. It was never discussed between us, but rather mutually assumed (because our friends did the same) that I would only make a brief appearance at the end. This kid was technically half mine and as a result, so were the gifts. Unfortunately, my *half* held the responsibility of carrying *all* the gifts. Aside from that, the only other downside to this shower was that I had to spend forty-five minutes showering, primping, and ironing a shirt.

I showed up at our friend Amber's house (hostess with the mostess) to kiss cheeks and dole out hugs as they were on their way out the front door. What I didn't see coming, was that I was left to help clean up the food and wrapping-paper carnage from thirty women—in my dress clothes, no less. I really felt that I should've been able to show up in sweats and a tanker, considering that, after recycling trash, collecting folding chairs, and sweeping up after the high tea, I'd be drenched like I just did a PX90 workout in church clothes. I had to spend an hour loading my vehicle with a half-ton of shit that would end up getting returned anyway.

Trying to avoid this when we registered ended up being a waste of time. We had doubles and triples of everything. Why, you ask? Because my wife secretly likes to return shit. The trait has somehow burrowed its way into her DNA. Before the registry hit the airwaves, she intentionally hopped online and rigged the list. There is no clear rhyme or reason, and I've given up trying to find one.

Personally, I don't return anything. I don't know if it's because I'm lazy or just because I'm a dude. If I buy something that doesn't fit or work for my cause, I toss it into the garage or give it to someone I know who might be able to use it. I once went through this delusional phase where I insisted I was a thirty-five waist when I was really a thirty-six. I also had myself convinced that I could fit into a large instead of an extra-large, only to get home from the mall with severe groin chaffing from skintight jeans and my belly peeking out from under a shirt of inadequate length. I'm constantly sizing people up that come over for dinner. "Are you a large? You look like a large," or insisting they try on a wool blazer that's completely out of season.

When we got home from Amber's, I unloaded the bulk of the gifts and added them to the sloppy pyramid in the dining room. It had started to worm its way into the hallway and was affecting foot traffic to and from the bedrooms and common areas.

As we were getting down to the wire, something needed to be done.

CHICKS LOVE CAR SEATS

The week before the delivery, I stayed late at my office, tying up loose ends on some TV pilot episodes we were shooting for Borderline Amazing, Chelsea Handler's company. I spent my nights after work breaking down that Tetris-sized formation in the dining room. Since "Adrian's Museum of Toys & Memorabilia" had been torn down and the nursery was now finished, we could distribute some of these gifts to their appropriate destination. At the bottom of the pile, I found something fairly important. Sure, it was the cornerstone to the wobbly pyramid, but it was also our car seat.

More than likely, my subconscious had intentionally buried this thing deep in the corner because I didn't want to force it into my car too early. I recently splurged and bought a new Audi SUV, my first really nice car. I had worked hard for it. Its sexy lines, panoramic moonroof, and thunderous concert bass could all be devalued by a hot chick in a nano-second with a car seat poking its ugly head out from the back-seat.

Another reason I held off on this was because I thought it would be simple and easy to install. I could drop it in on the fly when Jen finally called it off from our checklist, which is exactly what happened.

"What is that you're holding?" she asked. "You don't have the car seat in your car yet? What exactly were you waiting for?" she said.

I really didn't want to share my fantasy-based insecurities about picking up fake women at intersections, so I gave the standard "I don't know" with accompanying shoulder shrug and palms toward the sky.

"You should probably get out there and figure it out, in case she comes early. Don't you think?"

Early? I hadn't even considered this. WTF? Now I was a goddamned nervous wreck. How could she say something like that?

Our daughter had been breech and transverse almost the entire pregnancy. Aside from the doctor giving a try at ma-neuvering her, this was probably going to be a scheduled C-section. Nevertheless, I felt the pressure to get this opera-tion up and running.

"I'll be back in a minute," I said to her.

An hour later, I paced around the vehicle. I had all four car doors and the back hatch open, manuals strewn across the pavement and an ignored, stagnant cup of coffee parked in the grass with dead gnats floating in it. Neighbors walking their dogs were now pausing to contribute advice, along with every tenant coming in and out of the parking garage.

The last time I'd seen or dealt with a car seat was pretty much never. I thought you just threw this thing in the backseat and dropped the seat belt over it like a Friday-night bender buddy. Clearly, this was not the case.

I was involved in a calculated game of "find the anchor point," diving in and out of opposite sides of the car, fingering the European upholstery like a third date, looking for these goddamned elusive G-spot latches. Once I found them, we ramped up to climax as I contended with the adaptor, leveling dials, and adjustment heights.

This was fucking insane. Was I gonna have to go back and hit some night classes at the community college or enroll at a technical institute to get this thing figured out or what?

I adjusted the shoulder straps using my childhood teddy bear as a test dummy and got it to the point where both myself and Barrington were comfortable and satisfied with my handiwork.

Now the only thing left was to initiate some safety tests. I pushed, pulled, punched, and shoved this seat with all my might from every angle to simulate an accident. If my neighbors had something to comment on before, then they really had a field day as I went twelve rounds in the backseat of my car.

I fought a good fight, but the car seat won by decision.

CHAPTER 2

Wombsday

SOMEONE TAKE ME
TO THE HOSPITAL

Jen and I were lucky enough to have both sets of parents in town for the evacuation of her uterus, along with a few brothers and sisters from each side. The night before the delivery, I actually slept well, despite everyone telling me this was the end of sleep as I knew it.

The morning of the main event, I didn't have time to dick around, trying to get everyone together in a big rental car caravan to the hospital. Between my father-in-law stopping for a Misto and my mom having to find a restroom every ten minutes, I told them we would meet up at the hospital.

This particular day was something unique. This was the last time that Jen and I would be alone together as a couple for a long time. No more sleeping in or watching movies in thunderous surround sound late at night. The days of lying around on the sofa, leisure reading, playing gin rummy, or having romantic candlelight dinners for two were gone, at least for now. Much like Lord Dark Helmet chasing Captain Lone Starr and Barf, we skipped over hyperspace and went from light speed straight to plaid.

We rode in the car, soaking up Top Forty, enjoying a few last moments before this profound life change. Yes, I was nervous. And yes, I was driving like my late aunt Polly, bless her heart.

There were a few summers in my childhood where Polly drove my brothers and me to her shore house in New Jersey. She would white-knuckle the wheel of her canned pea–green Pontiac with both hands, her face pushed into the windshield, trying to see through her smudged Coke-bottle prescription glasses. She'd hover ten or fifteen miles below the speed limit in the right-hand lane of the interstate and, with no concern for time, intentionally take us well out of our way across another state line.

She used to think it was the neatest thing that I'd be able to go back to school in September and tell people that I was in Maryland for the first time, even if it was only for ten minutes.

And here I was, driving like my late great-aunt Polly on the 405, the busiest freeway in the country. We might not have even left the county, but mentally, I was certainly in a different state.

"I can't believe this is happening," I said, staring at Jen in the passenger's seat. How I meant it and how it was interpreted when it came out of my mouth were light-years apart. Right then and there I realized the importance of inflection.

At first, I didn't realize that what I said could've been perceived in two extremely different ways. As she scrunched her nose and squinted her brows together, I quickly backpedaled, sounding like Porky the Pig trying to spit out his infamous "Bedeebadeeb, th-th-that's all folks," attempting to explain exactly what I meant before she wasn't the only one checking into the hospital.

ME: Jenny, what I intended was that this was a giant leap . . . like . . . it's one of those landmark moments in life.

JEN: I'm glad you decided to go that route. And on a side note, I'm really relieved to hear that you're excited.

ME: Oh yeah, I'm definitely excited.

JEN: I've just always known that I was meant to have children, ya know? Almost like I was meant to be a mom. I dreamed about it as a child. Don't you feel the same way? Like you were meant to be a dad?

I pondered the question and how I might answer so that I didn't set this delivery off on the wrong foot. No sense in starting the game behind the eight ball. I thought to myself . . . Did I dream about being a dad when I grew up? Not really. I mean, maybe that's a girl thing.

I dreamed about one day taking Daisy Duke out on a date and feeling up her boobs in back of the General Lee. I dreamed about being an astronaut, wrestling in the WWF, or having a cool helicopter named *Airwolf.*

JEN: Well, didn't you?

ME: I don't know that I dreamed about it a lot, but I
             thought eventually someday I might be some
             kid's dad.

I don't know if I had her sold on it, but it must've sufficed. After nine months of cohabitating with a pregnant woman, I should've known to think about what the hell I was saying before the words left my mouth. Next time.

The delivery had been scheduled at our last doctor's appointment, which gave me the advantage of being prepared but the disadvantage of counting down the moment. I had my act together. I'd downloaded the appropriate apps, like Sig Alert, and Weather and Google Earth, which would give me environmental conditions and an eye in the sky. If Karma was going to choose now to pick a fight with me, he'd better bring his A-game.

I had routes *and* alternate routes. Traffic jam? High-speed chase? Air-raid sirens? No worries. We'd take the sewer if need be. I checked construction and marathon schedules and whether or not Obama was going to be in town, which was always a shit-show. I printed up parking structure blueprints for Cedars-Sinai and researched whether or not I had to pay daily fees, valet, etc., to ensure speed and proficiency upon arrival.

I made myself look like a boss and appear that I had everything dialed in for the main event.

I had phone chargers, laptops, cameras, clothes, and half my medicine cabinet stuffed into a gallon Ziploc. Plus the Phillies newborn onesie just in case the photo opportunity presented itself.

We stepped into the elevator at the hospital and started to climb. There was a weird silence, as we stood there anxiously, staring at the metal doors with nothing to really say to each other. It was one of those Larry David moments, had only the elevator jammed and left us stranded for the delivery.

The doors jumped open and we stood there looking at each other, confused.

For the first time in my life (probably the last), I stopped to ask for directions on where to go to get this kid out of my wife.

We approached the window outside the maternity ward to show our IDs and check in, and just as I handed over my license, the invisible two-by-four came out of nowhere and caught me square in the face, just like when Spade hit Farley on the side of the road that day.

It suddenly became *real* quicker than instant oats. I felt like the passenger of a car that had just blasted through a guardrail, torpedoed off a cliff, and plunged into the ocean, fighting to undo my seat belt as images of my twenties montaged their way through my head. Happy hours on Sunset Boulevard and strip poker in the Hollywood Hills, one-night stands and surfing at sunrise. Tailgating at sporting events and string bikinis on the beach. I was floating across the sand, throwing a Frisbee with a cute girl, and as I went up for the grab, it hit me in the teeth.

"Sir? SIR? SIR!" the receptionist said, as I yanked myself out of a vertical coma and into reality.

"Can you follow me down the hall, or do we need an orderly to put you on a gurney?" she asked.

Fucking smart-ass. Just because she's a callous blister from doing this for twenty-five years didn't mean she couldn't offer me a smidge of compassion on my first run.

From the check-in station, she led us down the hall into a prep room. Jen was assigned to a team of nurses and I was basically ignored. They asked her to strip down and get into her gown, attached her to an IV, double-checked family illness history, and interviewed her about her relationship with the father. That's me. Or at least that's the assumption we'd been operating under for the last nine months.

The nurse spoke softly while interviewing Jen, which immediately made me paranoid that they were talking about me. I acted like I couldn't hear them, but I was completely dialed in to what they were saying. Fortunately, my wife normally talks like she just got out of a metal concert where she was stuck next to the speaker all night. So I quickly understood the gist of the conversation.

The nurse leaned in and asked if she was in a physically abusive relationship. For the record, it's protocol to ask that question. It's not like she walked in there with two black eyes trying to have a kid.

For the rookie jokesters out there looking to lighten the mood, my advice would be to avoid the temptation to say "She wouldn't get hit if she kept her mouth shut." That kind of crack might fly around your best friends who know you're kidding, but this wasn't the time, nor the place.

My wits were about me, so I kept the blue material until later. After they wrapped up the social work session, the nurse tossed me a jumpsuit and a bag for my valuables.

Soooo . . . what? I'm gonna dump my new handcrafted leather wallet and iPhone into this bag and then throw it on the cart that "might" make it to recovery? No way. I saw the *Seinfeld* episode where Jerry's dad gets his wallet stolen at the doctor's office. I wasn't about to interrupt the best day of my life by jumping around the hallway like Morty, yelling, "My wallet's gone! My wallet's gone!"

By this time, our family had arrived, so I handed the goods over to my dad. I stuffed some cash into my sock, one of his classic moves from my childhood when we went into Philly for a ball game. Nobody was gonna jack my old man for his hard-earned cash, and the same went for me.

The jumpsuit lacked a bit of style, but this wasn't fashion week. What did concern me was the purpose of this whole ensemble. Was it a sterility thing, or was I gonna get messy in there?

The valuables were secure with the old man and the camera was the only thing left. Maybe I should've mounted this thing to a helmet. How was I going to carry it and keep it on the ready with no pockets?

Turns out, I used the wrist strap for the very first time. I'd never been a fan. I kind of thought they were a tad dainty. When I was a kid, my aunt used one when she came to visit on my birthdays, and without fail she would forget it was on her wrist while cutting cake, dragging it through the icing. We would spend the rest of the party talking about it. It was a bit emasculating for me, but today was a day of "man ups," so I put on my big-boy camera, let it slink down my forearm, and got ready to follow our posse out of the room.

DELIVERANCE

The prep room door opened and we began the voyage to the operating room. It might have been fifty feet or five hundred miles. I wouldn't have noticed the difference. Time had slowed down, and my anxiety was mounting. The OR doors buzzed open, and as I followed behind Jen and our entourage, the last nurse turned abruptly to me.

"You have a seat right here while we prep your wife. The environment needs to be kept semisterile," she said. In layman's terms, it meant they didn't want me in there cutting farts or sneezing pieces of my breakfast onto their surgical tools, and I could respect that.

She pointed to a lonely chair outside the double doors. The hallway ran an eternity in both directions, completely barren and void of any signs of civilization. As I sat in the cold corridor, left alone with my thoughts, I removed my wrist strap, turned the camera on myself, hoping to capture the pure fear and anxiety with the portrait setting of the camera. Bingo! I nailed it.

Aside from the chair I was in, the only other thing in the hallway was a wheelchair. I assumed it was there for my wife as a precaution, or for me, in the event that I blacked out and pancaked my head on the tile floor. I probably wouldn't be the first dad-to-be, nor the last, this happened to.

My mind began to wonder. My eyes went vacant, and I zoned out on the wheelchair. I daydreamed about how much fun it was for Cole Trickle and Rowdy Burns to race each other through the halls of the hospital in *Days of Thunder*. I thought about how the hammer was about to drop, not to help me pass the leader on the outside of turn four to win Daytona, but rather on me, to be a dad.

I heard some clanking of the surgical tools and became overly paranoid that maybe they forgot about me waiting in the hallway. Was that possible? Whose responsibility was I? What if someone was having a rough day at work and left me out here to rot?

Finally, one of the double doors squeaked open, a nurse instructed me to come in and showed me where to go. I tried my best to take in the surroundings, but making my way to the stool next to Jen's head was the immediate focus. I couldn't apathetically lumber in there, tripping over tubes or dragging my wristband camera across an open incision. PAY. AT-TENTION.

As I got comfortable (hardly) and gave my wife a "how's it going?" she already seemed a little loopy. "How's it going" probably wasn't the smoothest icebreaker and my "inflection" probably came off a bit smart-alecky. My eyes wandered around with everything that was going on. I knew we were in L.A., but still, we were in a hospital operating room and there were some overtly trendy nuances that caught my eye.

First, our anesthesiologist, who from here on out will be referred to as Randy Jackson, threw me a "Yo dawg," accompanied with an air-fist pound, then asked if I had brought my iPod. Hold the bus. Was I supposed to bring my fucking iPod? I had made my lists. Hell, I had made lists for the lists and followed them to a T. I thought I'd prepared for this special day with *everything*. He then followed up by asking if I had a birthing mix I wanted to use.

Holy shit, man, a birthing mix? Was this dude serious, or was he just messing around because I was the new guy? I've been painting a nursery, doing birth registry returns, and working full-time, my man. When in the hell did I have time to cut a mix together? He told me not to sweat it, as he had something that might work.

So there it was. We didn't have a mix. What *losers*.

Randy went ahead and plugged his iPhone into the dock. This cat had a mix ready to go. Who has a birthing mix carved out, ready to drop at any given moment? Our anesthesiologist, Randy Jackson, that's who. What were we about to be subjected to? I wasn't familiar with this guy's tastes. Could Jen give birth while listening to Nas or Rage Against the Machine?

We lucked out and shared the same taste in music. As Thom Yorke from Radiohead whined in with "Fake Plastic Trees," I admired the new Air Jordans on the feet of the tech running the vitals machine and the gauged earrings and neck tattoo on the orderly. If it weren't for the operating table and medical accoutrement, I'd swear we were at an after-hours party downtown.

A few minutes went by, and I could tell things were getting serious at a rapid pace. Before I knew it, our Wizard of Oz, Dr. Adberg, popped her head out from behind the curtain and gave me a rubber-gloved thumbs-up to start recording.

My first attempt at standing up indicated that I had a bad case of "accident legs."

That's when you're driving, almost get into an accident, and temporarily lose any feeling in your legs to pins and needles. They were cooked noodles.

I plopped back down on my stool and steadied myself to make another attempt, this time with Randy feeding me an inspirational "You got this, bro" and spotting me from behind.

Once again, the onslaught of invisible two-by-fours to the face continued, my mouth agape like I was catching flies at the fair, trying to steady the camera as a little person was yanked out of my wife's stomach. There was screaming and blood (not mine), but I wasn't worried because I had my jumpsuit on. My daughter drowned out Coldplay on the iPod dock and time came screeching to a stop.

Nine months of buying Cheetos and Bagel Bites (her pickles and ice cream), being shoved out of the bed by a body pillow the size of a hay bale, and having to pull the car over every five minutes to find a bathroom because my wife's bladder was being crushed were all suddenly worth it.

I was speechless. There haven't been too many times in my life where that's happened. In fact, sometimes you have to pay to get me to shut up. It's hard to imagine the power of this moment until you're actually there to experience it.

Within seconds, time sped back up and the room was

alive. There were fifteen people, a veritable pit crew, coming at our baby from the left and right, suctioning, wiping, and polishing. Each person had a job. They were clamping this and checking that, and the air suddenly got still as they handed me scissors and asked if I was going to cut the cord.

Along with not composing a birthing mix, I had also forgotten about this. I didn't think I was going to have the opportunity. Was I going to do this? This was weird.

On a regular vaginal delivery, I would've cut the cord as it was still attached to the mom, but on a C-section, they do it for you. I'm guessing they don't want you fumbling around over an open incision, dropping stuff inside, so they do the initial cut, but leave a little extra so that you still get the experience.

There wasn't any time to look around for my cojones, so I nodded and waited for them to steady the cord, pinch off, and tee me up with a scissor lane. We weren't snippin' some extra shoelace off your gym sneaker. This was the lifeline between mother and child for the last nine months. Instead of a few short strokes like I was making a construction-paper heart, I went with one big cut, like the newly inaugurated mayor cutting the town ribbon.

I managed to get the entire delivery on film, and I know this was important to my wife. I got pictures of the clock, the scale, the Air Jordans, neck tattoos, and hell, I even had Randy shoot me cutting that cord. I recorded my baby's first sounds and snapped a shot of the operating room staff.

I rocked out all of the most important things, or so I had thought. I was so preoccupied with "the moment" and maintaining consciousness that I didn't realize Jen hadn't held her own baby yet. It took my wife, strapped to a table, gargling words through vomit to remind me.

They finished cleaning up the baby, burritoed her in a soft blanket, and handed her to me. As I held my daughter in my arms for the very first time, I couldn't believe we (mostly my wife) had done it. We had brought a beautiful girl into this world. She was gorgeous. She was so small and fragile, I was nervous about holding her.

I leaned her down close to her mommy, and my wife began to cry. It's one of those extraordinary moments in life that can't be mimicked or re-created on any level. It's the purest, most emotional thing I've ever experienced.

As I held her tight and looked into her eyes, I realized that for months it had been my wife's job, but now I was her protector. It was now my job to help nurture, guide, and provide.

I was a dad.

IN MODERATE PAIN

One of the initial benefits of being a dad, aside from not having to shoot a kid out of my vagina, was being able to walk into the lounge and deliver the news to the anxious family waiting in the lobby.

For the first time since conception, I felt like I was part of the process. For nine months, Jen had helped plan her baby shower, bought new maternity clothes, and got regular exams. She was focused on a healthy diet, and her expanding tummy was the main topic of conversation. Sure, the guys at work knew my wife was expecting, but it didn't get that much airplay. Maybe that's just how it is.

I hadn't really thought about how I was going to make my big entry. I paused for a minute before slamming the big square button that opened the double doors into the waiting room. Should I give them the classic "stick 'em up" with guns drawn or the "arms in the air" quarterback celebration after he throws the game-winning Hail Mary?

I went with the quarterback. I stormed the room with my arms up, waited to be spotted, and yelled, "It's a girl!" even though we'd already known that for six months. What they didn't know was the name. I told them we had decided on Ava. As Jen lay in the other room almost torn in half, hooked up to machines, and blasted on painkillers, I was the man.

It was kind of unfair. I didn't even really do anything. After years of trying to prevent this debacle, I broke the streak one Friday night and used my penis to its ultimate potential. After that, I sat back and relaxed for three quarters of a year, then drove us over here.

I can't complain, however, about how great of a moment it was. Everyone hugged, mobbed, and congratulated me like I had thwarted a terrorist attack and saved the country. Facebook updates, phone calls, and tweets were being delivered as I kicked back and tucked cigars into my shirt pocket.

I ducked out to the transitioning room (between the OR and our permanent recovery room), where Jen was being monitored and the baby was sleeping soundly. I was already exhausted, and all I'd done was hold Jen's hand, take some pictures, and do an end zone dance in the waiting room. I was depleted and could've used my own saline bag to bring me back. There wasn't any time for a nap, though, as family members were frothing at the mouth to get back to us and visit.

We were moved to our recovery room, and within five minutes, the exodus from the lobby began, two by two, back to visit us and meet the newest member of our family.

Since shelling out twenty-five hundred dollars (some

hospitals have special rooms) a night to get a suite wasn't an option, we were assigned to a regular recovery room. When I say it was "pretty tight," you'll learn to appreciate the understatement.

There was an adjustable bed, an IV stand, and a rocking chair. In the corner, for me, sat a folded-up aluminum postpartum cot, hereafter known as the iron maiden, held together with a dime-store bungee cord.

There weren't too many choices about where to unfurl and display my bed. Conveniently, the only real area was directly below a dry-erase board that needed to be updated every half hour by one of the dozens of rotating nurses we had during our stay.

There wasn't any potpourri or a jet spa in the bathroom. Instead, a bag of mesh underwear for my wife and a rip cord hanging next to the crapper that you could pull on if you got into any trouble.

It wasn't long before everyone who had come to visit had squeezed me out of the room. I'm sure the staff often looks the other way when you've exceeded your capacity of visitors. So long as no one was rolling a beer ball in, they left us alone. After the nurses brought us to recovery, they read us the riot act about germs. I was absolutely paranoid about the situation and set up a mock checkpoint at the door, feeling early-onset carpal tunnel, pumping out Purell for everyone going in and out.

When I wasn't working a shift as a maternity bouncer, I was butlering. Opening Jell-O, changing the baby, signing for gifts and flowers, and obsessively rearranging everything within our limited space on a regular basis.

Next to the bed, on the wall, was a laminated one sheet,

entitled "Wong-Baker pain scale." It was a placard with a series of emoticons and a specific feeling attached to each one. As the nurses continued their half-hourly rampage, a new assessment accompanied each visit and was recorded in Jen's file.

I studied the scale and made an evaluation of my own. Seems that I fell into "moderate pain" for most of my stay. During the day, we sat in our cell around the clock, watching standard-definition local television and eating tepid takeout from the night before.

I was six one, two hundred twenty pounds, and the "iron maiden" was close to meeting its match. I broke three springs on the first night and woke the baby up twice, peeling my skin from the plastic mattress. There was a nurse in our room every fifteen minutes, bumping her knee into my hospital wood so she could squeaky-scribble on the dry-erase board above my body. There was nothing more comforting than to wake up with someone hovering over you, clawing at the wall with a marker.

With visitors coming in and out during the day, I found myself stepping away for a minute, ruling the halls in my robe like a hospital Hefner. By day two, it felt like old hat. I made my rounds, exchanging gossip with Phyllis in the gift shop and bullshitting about the Lakers with Greg, the cafeteria cashier.

Aside from a psych ward or a college dorm, I wasn't sure where else you would be allowed to walk around all day in your pajamas and not catch shit for it. Not only were people not coming down on me, they were hitting me with high-fives and "congrats." The slippers and wristband identified me as a new dad, a man of the hour.

Some people might think it's difficult to have house-guests for the weekend, but I'll go ahead and assure you that this was more painful, sharing a ten-by-ten room every day with friends and family.

Don't get me wrong. We were extremely lucky to have that many people who cared about us, and I would never diminish the importance of that. But by the end of the first day, it looked like the remnants of a fraternity party. Starbucks floaters, boob pads used as coasters, and somewhere, hidden under an In-N-Out hamburger wrapper, the baby.

That second night, I had a little surprise for Jen. One night at dinner with friends, a few weeks before her due date, jokes had been flying around the table. They had teased about the fact that I had probably overlooked the "baby bauble," its street name being the "push present."

At the time, I smirked and nodded like I had it covered, but the truth was that I had overlooked it. I had no idea what in the hell they were talking about. Wasn't the baby the gift?

My interpretation from a consensus of my buddies revealed that your wife is giving *you* the gift of a child, so you should go out and find something to give to *her*.

Fear of falling short of the social norm (and her friends gossiping) sent me out on a mission. Most women rarely get sick of seeing a jewelry box, so when she went to the bathroom before bed, I quietly placed a little box next to her chicken broth and cafeteria dinner roll.

As she unraveled the package and uncovered the opal (birthstone of our daughter) and diamond earrings, any recent shortcomings were wiped off the chalkboard. The two opals represented her and Ava's birthdays, and the diamonds were a metaphor for my testicles. Instead of in a jar up on the mantel, I felt they were better displayed fixed to her ears.

On day three, there was a knock at the door. I assumed it was my father-in-law and brother-in-law, who had gone downstairs on a coffee mission. Instead, it was an older black woman.

And this is how that conversation went:

ME: Can I help you?

HER: I'm the lactation specialist.

ME: What's this now?

HER: I'm here to see your wife. Is she doing okay with her milk?

ME: Yeah, I think she's all good. I got her some from the cafeteria.

HER: No, her breast milk.

ME: Oh.

Well. This was somewhat unexpected. This stranger was there to help Jen with her breastfeeding techniques. This was one of those things that I had no clue about. She was accompanied by a hospital liaison, who informed me that all new moms get a visit from this woman, who is an expert with instructing on "holds" and how to get your baby to latch properly onto the breast. Perhaps I could also personally benefit from her advice, so I decided to pay close attention.

I quickly discovered that I was out of my league on this one and hit the sidelines as my mom, mother-in-law, and this random lady I had just met all huddled around my wife's boobs. They were hauled out posthaste, wobbling around in circles like a pair of drunken, veiny Cyclopes, being banged around, tugged at, and honked on like a clown horn.

For some reason, this made me uncomfortable. My father-in-law, his brother, and my brother-in-law had now strolled in with lattes, and I'd quickly ushered them back into the hallway before we had a half-dozen people hanging out, having a fireside chat, while my wife's knockers were getting worked over by a team.

By the end of that third day, I didn't care how great this hospital was or what celebrities went here, I was ready to get the hell out. I'd had my fill of cafeteria egg burritos and aged vending machine snacks.

T minus twelve hours and I'd be at home, laid out on my leather sofa, watching something on cable in high-definition. As I looked around the room, I wondered how in the hell I was going to get all this shit back to our place. The math was killing me.

Problem: What is 20 vases + 30 gifts × 7 floors and a parking garage?

Answer: FAIL.

I also started to question when this kid was going to wake up. So far her repertoire included breathing, sleeping, and diapers with extra Dijon mustard.

By the fourth morning, I was chomping at the bit, ready to go. I'd had my fill of one-ply toilet paper and the iron maiden. The night before, I had packed everything up that I possibly could, and now it was just a few formalities that lay between me and sitting on my own toilet.

Jen was handling the exit paperwork and getting the Baby LoJack removed while I loaded up a maintenance cart to make a run to the car.

The LoJack was an anklet that got attached to the baby immediately after she left the operating room. If the anklet breaches the entrance to the maternity ward, alarms activate and the entire place goes on lockdown.

The United States has been using these for quite some time now, but it makes me wonder what happened before they were implemented. Maybe you should wonder, too, the next time you're visiting those people you've been calling your parents all these years.

As the nurse came in to remove the device and we unburritoed Ava from her swaddle, we made a fun discovery. There was no device.

Somehow, the little worm had kicked it off. A frantic search by mom and staff revealed that it was stuffed down in between her blanket and the bassinet. After a mild freak-out from everyone in the room, we determined that our bands still matched up and we weren't victims of the ol' switcheroo.

An orderly brought the maintenance cart up to the room for me to remove our gifts and take them to the car. As I maneuvered through the halls toward the elevator with clanking glass and flowers, I couldn't help but feel like Hef was dead.

I was without robe and void of that new baby virgin excitement on my face. I was malnourished and weak, staggering back and forth like a stooge, struggling to keep this busted-ass cart going in a straight line without losing any lilacs or cookie arrangements. My, how the mighty have fallen.

DEMOLITION DERBY

A new panic had now hit me. We were leaving the hospital, and as much as I had bitched about having a nurse in our room every half hour, the bottom line was that they were the highest-paid babysitters we would ever have, and from here on out it was up to us to keep this child alive.

A volunteer brought the girls down to the parking garage in a wheelchair (mandatory) to make sure I wasn't having them jump in the back of a pickup truck to head out. She had to verify that not only did we have a car seat, but that it was installed properly. I was more than happy to show her my handiwork, and upon inspection, she nodded at me and smiled, her way of letting me know that I'd done a good job. I insisted that she tug at the anchor points and give it a good back 'n' forth to confirm its stability. She seemed only mildly impressed, but I wore the moment like a badge of achievement.

We were beyond excited to go home for the first time as a new family. I filled the front seat and the back of our car with bags, vases, and gifts. I had everything packed in snug, so no expired flower water would hit the rugs. Jen rode in the back with Ava. We chose some soothing lullabies and achieved the optimal cabin temperature for the baby. We exchanged a true moment of relief, exhaled, and smiled at each other.

I put the car in drive, and we made it about twenty feet before some wacko in an SUV hammered on the gas while backing out of her spot and slammed into a parked car directly in front of us, blocking our exit.

Holy shit. Did she just annihilate a parked car? That could've been us. The woman, clearly panicked, hopped out of the car, dancing around and waving jazz hands in the air like some sort of lunatic. Ava was now crying and, by golly, if we didn't have a goddamned situation going down.

My in-laws had also been getting in their car, which was close enough for them to hear the action, and came running. The driver was so flustered that she couldn't get back behind the wheel. My father-in-law had to move her car back into her original parking space and instruct her on what to do next. She was the black cat I was trying to avoid on the maiden voyage home with an infant in the car.

If I wasn't on edge then, I certainly was now. I never took notice before, but everyone on the road, specifically in L.A., drives like a complete asshole. I felt like a slow-motion Indiana Jones behind the wheel of a truck packed with wet dynamite and angry Germans whizzing by on the left and right trying to run me off the road.

There was no more steering with my knee while talking on my cell phone. No more rubbernecking the landscapes or playing with the iPod. I stayed in the middle lane, both hands (first time ever) on the wheel at ten and two, chewing on my tongue so as to not swallow it in a panic, while uninsured motorists and undocumented immigrants zipped by me with middle fingers hanging out the window.

Jen tried to remain calm in the backseat, holding Ava's hand, but inevitably there were things for her to point out. Avoiding potholes, merging on and off the freeway, and getting home without a wreck was no easy task.

Welcome home, Dad.

CHAPTER 3

One Step Forward, Three Steps Back

IN THE DOGHOUSE

We did make it home safely without further incident. The days of eating out of vending machines and recycling my underwear by turning them inside out were over. No longer would I have to touch my derriere to a foreign toilet seat, watch sporting events in standard definition, remember the names of dozens of rotating nurses, or drink freeze-dried instant coffee when the Starbucks was closed.

My mother-in-law had fixed a giant pink bow to the door of our apartment to welcome us home. We were lucky enough to have her stay with us for a week or two to help out.

I don't believe the bow is just a Southern tradition, as I'd seen them before. It served as a general declaration to the neighborhood: We just had a baby girl! So don't think about coming over to borrow cream or sugar for the next few weeks unless you want to get stuck babysitting.

It took me several trips, but I managed to lug all of the gifts and flowers upstairs and inside. I imagine that normal people keep baby gifts and congratulatory arrangements around for a week or so, simply to display and enjoy them. Then they either utilize the gift, put it on a shelf, or toss whatever might be perishable. Evidently we didn't fall within society's definition of "normal."

The elaborate cookie bouquets were to remain untouched, and my wife's restraining order dictated that I was not to breach the plastic wrap. I couldn't even get near them. The fluffy shortbread cookies were perfectly iced and thoughtfully plugged into pink, spray-painted Styrofoam adorned with confetti creations. Aside from being a gift we received for her birth, I couldn't explore their alternate value, satisfier of the sweet tooth. It's not like they were governmentally protected monolithic stone statues from Easter Island or one of the Seven Wonders of the Ancient World. They were fucking cookies . . . delicious, mouthwatering cookies. As I eventually found out, when Jen said "not just yet," it meant "never." I watched painfully as the arrangements moved from the "best by" to "no longer edible" category. At the end of the day, I really just think that my wife wanted to stay in the moment forever, and these cookies happened to be the ambassador of Ava's birth.

They were admired and photographed for a long time, but after eight months, they were nothing more than concrete discs that had no business going in my mouth. I'll never know what they tasted like and still experience night terrors after being forced to lay them to rest in the Dumpster.

Not having a full-time nursing staff around made itself apparent within the first hour we were home. As much as I complained, those nurses were always there to give recommendations, offer advice, and even take the baby to the nursery if we wanted to try to sleep for an hour.

The tandem rides were over. The training wheels busted off as we flew down parenting hill. This was game on, and it was our turn to shine. We had a towering stack of baby books to reference, but half of them were so painfully boring that I couldn't bear to spend a minute reading them. The other half spoke specifically to new mothers, leaving fathers in the dark. Which is partially why I'm writing this book today.

With help from the maternity nurses, we'd gotten into a decent routine at the hospital and carried it over as best we could once we got home. But there were things other than a schedule and feedings to contend with.

Before we considered having children, Jen had made the suggestion that we get a dog. I couldn't help but think that this was some trendy idea she saw on morning television, where some "expert" claimed that raising a pet together as a couple would serve as a practice run for having a child.

I'd had a Golden Lab named Cara while growing up, and my parents had placed the responsibility on me to raise her. I enjoyed it then, a boy and his dog in the country. There was something poetic about it. We palled around together, running through the creek and playing fetch in the yard. She used to follow me as I mowed the lawn and was great at alerting us when the Jehovah's Witnesses were coming up the driveway. Sounds nice, right?

But that's when I was thirteen. My responsibilities were very limited and I had time to do this. I could put *Contra* or *The Legend of Zelda* on pause. When I was in my early thirties, this sounded like a headache, but if this was what it was going to take to prove to Jen that I could be a good dad, and we agreed to share the responsibility, then so be it.

We'd driven out to Cherry Valley, about one hundred miles east of Los Angeles. We found a quaint little farm online that was a licensed Boston terrier breeder and sat down in their living room to acquaint ourselves with two new litters totaling thirty puppies. We were fond of the runt—one black eye and one white eye. He was particularly playful and ultimately irresistible, so we took him home and named him Cooper.

Then we worked on getting him potty trained. For the first few weeks, we shared the burden of taking him out to pee, poop, and get some much-needed exercise.

With the dog parenting a success, the path was paved for us to have kids. Once pregnant, Jen let me know that she was no longer able to pick up poop. She had read an article online that cat poop could be a danger to the fetus and went ahead and lumped dog crap into the same category. How convenient. After a few weeks of solo scooping, I wanted to find the guy who'd written this article and tie a bag around his head filled with dog shit, drive him to my house, and make him tell my wife he was a liar and his findings were based only on a small case study.

There was no sense in arguing with her while she was pregnant, but come August, I'd be delivering my own research on the topic, along with a formal letter of reinstatement to crap collection.

From here on out, and to this day four years later, "dog caretaker" is one of my many hats. Let this be a lesson to any guys reading this who are being convinced to get a soft, lovable, cuddly puppy before you have kids. You've been warned.

We had Cooper for a little over a year before Ava was born and hadn't necessarily considered the implications involved with introducing this trend victim of a dog to a new baby in the household.

Up until that point, he was the center of our childless universe. We took him on road trips and he flew cross-country to visit family with us. We brought him to Boston terrier meet-ups at local dog parks, and Jen dressed him up in stupid sweaters and costumes on the holidays.

How was he going to react to the time- and emotional-suck that was a newborn? One of the nurses at the hospital told us to present him with one of Ava's diapers, to let him sniff it and become familiar with her scent.

To date, hundreds of chewed up and torn-apart full diapers that were accidentally left unattended have haunted my very being. This made me consider that while her intentions were probably good, this nurse owed me a few gift cards for the rug doctor.

The dog stood his ground and even occasionally lashed out. He stole pacifiers and stuffed animals and understandably had trouble acknowledging that Sophie the Giraffe, a soft, rubbery squeaky toy that appeared like the Holy Grail of dog toys, wasn't his. He regressed and rebelled, pissing and shitting all over the house. I went from having one kid in diapers to having a kid *and* a dog in diapers. Literally.

Yes, I gave up. I was at the end of my mental rope. You heard me correctly. I put my fucking dog in a diaper. I had enough on my plate with an infant and couldn't bear the burden of having to "spot shot" the rug every hour in half a dozen places.

Dire situations call for dire solutions.

Cooper was always curious and constantly investigating the baby. He never physically lunged at or tried to hurt Ava; in fact, if anything, he eventually took on the role of her protector.

With him constantly sniffing around though, I was very conscious about Ava's belly button. All newborns have their umbilical cord cut and clamped. The clamp is removed upon checkout of the hospital and the remaining cord eventually dries up and falls off.

With routine diaper changes and baths, the cord stump becomes loose, and this was the case with Ava. I didn't want it to fall off without us noticing. Not that I was going to put it in a Ziploc in the freezer or smash it between the pages of her baby book, I just didn't want it set free in the apartment, somehow managing to get stuck between my toes on a midnight walk to the bathroom.

One evening, while Jen and I were eating dinner, my mother-in-law had been cuddling with Ava on the sofa. At some point, I noticed the dog dive in between her and the couch, pick something up in his mouth, and take off to the other side of the room, beyond anyone's jurisdiction.

It took me a minute to realize what had happened. The cord had fallen off and Cooper was chomping away on it. Was this real life? Was this actually happening right now?

I alerted everyone as to what had just happened, and we fought back the collective urge to vomit. At that moment, with the dog in a diaper, hunched over in the corner, chowing down on an umbilical cord stub, I had lost my appetite.

SHE'S GONNA HAVE DADDY ISSUES

Within a few days of being home, it was time to take Ava for her first pediatrician visit. The doctor who saw her in the hospital after her birth needed to see her again . . . and again . . . and again. Between immunizations and well checks, we were there so often that I should've just had my mail forwarded to the pediatrician's office for the first few weeks.

When I was a kid, my mom was always better equipped to handle the doctor than my dad. This was probably because she was a nurse. My dad's kryptonite was screaming, germ-ridden kids (that weren't his), and perhaps it's genetic, because I wasn't far behind.

You would think a pediatrician's office in Beverly Hills would be some glamorous place with gold-leafed picture frames, massage chairs for the waiting parents and candy stripers peddling Purell like hors d'oeuvres.

As a child growing up in rural Pennsylvania, I always perceived Beverly Hills as an amazing wonderland of glitz and glamour. Watching Robin Leach fawn over the rich every week and Joan Rivers doing interviews on the red carpet led me to expect pretty spectacular things from this place.

I pulled into the underground garage and handed the keys over to a parking attendant while he helped me get the family out of the car. Only in L.A.

It would've been silly to valet your car at the pediatrician when I was a kid. If having an attendant park your car would've been necessary, we would've left it across the street at the supermarket and sprinted across the highway, screwing the valet attendant out of an opportunity to put a ding in my mom's Barracuda and take us for twelve bucks.

The building lobby was quiet, expensive bouquets and pristine marble floors. So far, my expectations were dead-on. That is, until we got upstairs.

I was wrong. Pediatrician offices are all the same. The "well" entrance was on the left and the "sick" entrance on the right, with hand sanitizer everywhere in between.

I nearly goofed and entered on the sick side by mistake. The few centimeters between my hand and the wrong doorknob were all that separated my fingers from caressing fecal matter and pink-eye spores. I froze, stopping dead in my tracks, with the stroller my wife was pushing, slicing into my Achilles. I carefully backed up and redirected us toward the healthy entrance with Jen realizing my mistake and letting a chuckle slip. She tends to think that I'm overly obsessive and excessively germaphobic. She was probably secretly rooting for me to touch that doorknob.

I turned the handle and opened the door to the waiting

room. There weren't any part-time thespians dressed up like germ mascots vying for photo ops with the kids; nor were there any Godiva "get well soon" lollipop trees.

Instead, it was a massive case of déjà vu.

I was drenched by a flood of childhood memories. It was all there. There was a fish tank, with a few tired tropical stragglers, a chalkboard with a few nubs of chalk that hadn't been eaten yet, and a gang of stuffed animals that looked like they'd fallen out of a pickup truck on the freeway. I located the sign-in sheet and prepared to stand until they called our name, because the two-seat bench meant to accommodate ten patients was occupied.

I was already in "let's get the hell outta here" mode and we'd been there for only five minutes. It was painful. Since Ava was only a few days old and newborns get priority, the nurse called us back right away. She came in to discuss the vaccine schedule, and Jen and I moved quickly from certainty to uncertainty.

We had discussed an alternative vaccination schedule for Ava. We didn't want to avoid any of the vaccinations, but were concerned (like many parents are) about giving so many in a short period of time to such a vulnerable little person. Fortunately, our pediatrician was comfortable with our decision, and the only downside was that we had to make more trips to this office as we broke down the schedule.

On this particular visit, Ava was supposed to get her first shot. We had discussed everything: which vaccination she was getting, which appendage it would be given to, and when we would come back for the next one. What we didn't discuss was how we were going to go about handling Ava during the process. We fought like Roseanne and Dan over who was going to hold her while the shot was being administered, and having the nurse standing there while we bickered amplified a simply wonderful experience.

We did rock, paper, scissors. Hot potato. Odds and evens. Thumb wars. We did everything short of arm wrestling for it. We finally settled for a vote.

Somehow, even though the vote was a split decision, I was nominated and elected. The bottom line was that neither of us wanted to have Ava associate either parent with pain. I certainly didn't want to be the bad guy, but since I was on a roll with manning up, it was time to stick with the theme, turn up my sleeves, and get dirty.

I really hoped this didn't have a domino effect. The first to be knocked over, triggering a pinwheel of rebellious decisions and actions made during adolescence, evolving her into a teenaged she-devil with daddy issues.

Dad's an asshole! Screw him. He hurt me as a baby!

The nurse had come back to figure out if we were done with our series of physical challenges to determine who was going to hold Ava. I begrudgingly stepped up to the plate. As she lay there, I held her tight and avoided any eye contact. The shot was administered, and I held on to the tiny mechanical bull for dear life.

She could hardly catch her breath, and after about ten seconds, let out a scream that could've shattered the windows like a sonic boom. The nurse slapped on a nude round Band-Aid and dipped out of the room. I didn't blame her.

"It's okay" and "Sssh, you'll be fine" were total crocks. I was already a scumbag liar. How did I get bamboozled into this?

I assumed that since I took the bullet on this one, that

Mommy would do her best to defend my actions and lessen the fear and animosity toward me. Instead, she swooped in with one of her giant Cyclops knockers, shoved it in Ava's mouth, and said things like, "Oh, honey, I know. Dada is mean, isn't he?" in a "The plane is going down, but remain calm" soothing-flight-attendant voice.

Not only did Jen get into Ava's good graces with her built-in food supply, but she was also still riding next to her in the backseat like Thelma and Louise, leaving me to chauffer them back home, fighting to keep my eyes open.

We weren't getting much sleep, having to feed and change Ava every three hours. Jen was on a paid maternity leave from her job as a reality-TV development executive, but my days were numbered. In less than a week, I'd have to go back to my job, doing essentially the same thing as Jen, but for Chelsea Handler. I needed to get some sleep. The unsolicited counsel we got from everyone in the weeks leading up to the birth was "Get your sleep now." I never understood what the hell they meant by that.

Was I going to accumulate and bank my sleep hours, only to pull them out and use them in the future when I really needed them? This advice sucked.

What about some advice I could actually use like "Coffee will be your best friend, so here's a Starbucks gift card" or "From now on, your laundry is fucked. Here's a Tide stain stick." At least that would've made some sense.

BREAST IN PEACE

There were a lot of changes I'd noticed in the first two weeks at home. Certainly the sleep deprivation connected with one a.m., three a.m., and five a.m. feedings, hourly diaper changes, and walking or rocking the baby to get her to stop crying. Another change was the physical and mental composition of my wife.

Once we got Dolly Parton home from the hospital, I noticed something wonderfully unusual. It was a fairy-tale dream come true. She was wearing loose tank tops with no bra and had these giant gentlemen's club knockers that whirled around the atmosphere like a carnival ride. It was so amazing. But with the good, comes the bad.

Just like those delicious cookie arrangements that were off-limits, so were these. I could look, but I could rarely touch. She claimed they were engorged (impossible to argue, rock on) and painful, so feelskis and motorboats were off-limits. I found myself swimming in a sea of trick bras with peekaboo access panels and a noisy piece of equipment called a breast pump.

When she wasn't feeding, she was pumping to bank milk for when she eventually went back to work. The breast pump is a bunch of tubes connected to suction cups, which were then connected to a little engine discreetly hidden within a "fashionable" tote bag. It also came with a special nursing bra, which looked like a weightlifting belt with areola holes cut out of it. It took the whole world of being a sexy dominatrix and somehow twisted and tangled it all up with dairy farming.

All of my friends and uncles disappeared when it was time to discuss the postpartum state of the union. It's a fragile existence, with hormone levels through the roof one minute and in the basement the next. I kept my head down. I minimized my opinions, observations, and thoughts and crawled through life on my stomach, trying not to get hit with an emotional backlash mortar.

Do what you're told, and don't stand up in the canoe or you're going to fall in and get wet.

I didn't bother figuring out the decision-making process:

ME: Hey, honey, I'm going to pick up the food. Is the order under your name?

JEN: Yeah, I ordered three different sandwiches because I'll probably want a bite or two of each one. Oh, and each one has a different sauce that I asked for on the side. Could you double-check to make sure they did it right?

ME: Cool! Sounds good!

And I didn't try and diagnose emotional irregularities either, even if I heard her uncontrollably wailing in the other room:

ME: Why are you crying? Is Ava okay? Did something happen to you or the dog?

JEN: The woman on this home improvement show went over budget and couldn't afford the brushed steel fixtures she wanted!

ME: Oh. Ahh, well . . . everything happens for a reason. I'm sure something great is just waiting to happen to her.

And after this encounter, I *really* steered clear of anything having to do with frivolous purchases or overspending:

ME: Jen? Do you know what all of these random fraudulent charges are on our account?

JEN: Like what?

ME: A two-foot shoehorn, bedazzled travel mug, and some decorative wooden bookshelf initials.

JEN: Yeah. I bought those. We needed that stuff.

What I should've said was that those definitely seemed like things we needed and I had only hoped to beat her to it.

Instead, I called her out and used phrases like "frivolous spending" and "moronic moves." I raised questions about the charges from the other room. I could've kept my head down, but instead I'd escalated it into a full-blown argument, with us meeting in the middle of the living room yelling at each other, my wife with a tote bag slung over her shoulder and a suction cup on each boob. I was disarmed by the deafening suctioning sound, and the whirring of the motor overpowered the discussion. Quite honestly, someone needs to contact the law enforcement agencies and let them know to start looking into using this technique as some sort of hostage negotiation tactic. I gave up, apologized, and walked away.

It took me a little while to get used to the idea that Jen would be breastfeeding in public. I didn't expect her to use the Hooter Hider or any other knockoff shower curtain fixed to her neck and draped around her body. However, I'd hoped she wouldn't act like this was Woodstock and practice a *little* discretion, either by using a scarf or maybe even a blankie to cover up the action.

In the first few weeks, I was always on my toes, making sure that if we were out in public, no creepers were bagging an eyeful at my wife's expense. To my surprise, most everyone seemed pretty normal about it. In fact, my wife argued that I was the one acting overly abnormal. Go figure.

What I began to understand was that breastfeeding was a natural function. It wasn't meant to be a montage of nip slips put together on a Joe Francis DVD. It was nourishing your offspring with immunities to help them live.

There were only one or two occasions where I had to pipe up and tell some dudes to "take a picture; it'll last longer," and I think it sufficiently embarrassed them to the point of not looking over at her again.

As time went on, we both became more comfortable with the whole practice, and today I honestly couldn't care less if she walked around topless on the Metro. So long as your wife is doing it, too.

KEEP LAUGHING, IT'S NOT THAT FUNNY

My days of hogging the boobs were over, just like my vacation from work. I'll admit that I was looking forward to a bit of a reprieve from the craziness of life with a newborn and excited about having some actual adult conversations that didn't require babies as the theme. My two weeks off were up, and I now had to return to my "other" grind.

Aside from being a tad exhausted, I was back in action as if everything were normal. Toward the beginning of my career in comedy, I had worked for Adam Sandler for almost eight years. I began as an assistant while we started a television production company within Happy Madison Productions and also co-ran his Web site, Adamsandler.com. I worked my way up to become a manager, then director, and eventually a VP of television development. We had just sold *Rules of Engagement* to CBS, which would go on to become a major success for the network.

While I worked at Sandler's Happy Madison, I simultaneously consulted as a comic booker for *The Late Late Show with Craig Ferguson*, also on CBS. During my tenure, I booked dozens of comics on the critically acclaimed late-night show.

I was a fixture in the comedy underground of Los Angeles. I spent my nights hopping back and forth between the Comedy Store and Laugh Factory on Sunset Boulevard, as well as the Hollywood Improv on Melrose. I was appointed to an advisory committee for the annual Aspen U.S. Comedy Arts Festival and judged comics at national and international comedy competitions.

A few months prior to Ava's birth, I had reached a point in my career where I felt like I needed to evolve and, after eight years, made a tearful departure from the Happy Madison family. My time there was one of the best experiences of my life.

I had taken a chance and left to become the VP of Development for Borderline Amazing Productions, the newly formed production company for Chelsea Handler, a fiery comedian and host of E!'s *Chelsea Lately*. We got along very well, and it was a perfect fit for me.

But I truly had my hands full. I was spread thin around my work responsibilities and didn't get to help out that much with Ava once I got home at night. I was just too exhausted.

For a kid raised in the farmlands of rural Pennsylvania, it was a bit surreal to have gifts come into the hospital from people like Adam, Chelsea, Heidi and Seal, actors, writers, and executives at major television networks and studios.

My friends and family were buzzing about everything—my new job and the addition to the family. I was riding high and getting into a groove, not only as a development executive, but as a father as well. I was trying to find a balance between work and home life, which proved difficult. I was leaving for work earlier in the morning, but also coming home a little sooner than I used to so I could catch dinner, give Ava a bath, and help put her down for bed.

I didn't necessarily grasp the entirety of what my wife was doing during the day. I wasn't sure how taking care of an infant alone could be a full-time job.

Not yet anyway.

FLY THE UNFRIENDLY SKIES

Ava was only two weeks old when Halloween rolled around, too young to egg and TP some houses or dress up and hit the streets, or so I had thought. We lived in a gated apartment complex by the beach at the time, and I figured we were safe from having to answer the door every five minutes for trick-or-treaters. If anyone dared to knock, I'd flip them a brick of frozen breast milk and tell them to be on their way.

I got home from work on Halloween night and was getting comfy on the sofa, ready to burn through some shows we still hadn't watched from our time away in the hospital. That's when Jen came into the living room wearing an *Eyes Wide Shut* mask with Ava dressed as a pea in a pod. She had the dog next to her, dressed up like a fairy princess, complete with wings and a sparkly halo. Our dog is a dude.

"Where are we going to trick or treat?" she asked.

"I don't know. It's L.A., it's eighty degrees outside, and we live in an apartment complex. Are we going to start knocking on doors in our hallway?" I replied.

Am I going to interrupt some twenty-two-year-old while he's smoking a bong to show him my pea pod and ask him to turn over his stoner snacks to my dog's pumpkin pail? I agreed to go, but *only* for a few minutes.

If anyone had asked why I wasn't dressed up, I'd simply say that these holidays were for the kids and I was focused on establishing an important tradition so that she didn't miss out on anything. This Halloween thing actually turned out to be a solid plan, as she was too young for candy. I would reap the benefits later that night after she went to bed, rooting through her stash to eventually piss my dentist off.

We met a few people in the courtyard, most of whom, instead of showing up with kids, also had dogs in costume (that's L.A. for you), taking the pressure off of us being the only assholes. We traded some Snickers, and before Ava got too restless, we went back upstairs. The whole process was actually relatively painless.

What wasn't painless was a few weeks later when we decided to take off for the Christmas and New Year's holiday. We stayed in town and had a low-key first Thanksgiving as a family but decided that we really needed to visit our parents, first in Atlanta, then Philadelphia, to celebrate Ava's first Christmas.

I had thought that packing our bags for a week's stay in the hospital was rough. That was amateur hour.

We had to gear up for three separate flights and three weeks in two different cities with a newborn and a dog. Flying the red-eye with an infant isn't nearly as glamorous as you might think, but it did have its perks.

Wait. No, it didn't. It didn't have *any* perks.

Welcome to being the disease. It was as if we were lepers, walking onto an overnight flight with a baby. No one wanted anything to do with us. I asked my brother to drive us to the airport so we could avoid having to take a newborn in a taxi. Something about the idea of strapping my car seat into the back of a cab just didn't sit well with me.

Because it took me forever to load up the vehicle, we arrived at the airport with only minutes to spare. I had four suitcases, two personal items, a carry-on, and a doggie duffel bag to get inside, along with Jen, who had Ava and the stroller.

I had met my match. Up until this point, I'd always been able to navigate my own way, unassisted, through the airport check-in process. My pride was already rattled as I worked to flatten and finesse crinkled single dollar bills into the Smarte Carte vending machine and run back curbside to load up my entourage.

After pleading with several airline employees, we finally located a supervisor and asked for help getting scooted to the front of a line to make this flight. I didn't even want to consider the alternative, since my brother was already long gone. As we pleaded our case, the Christmas spirit and overall compassion for our pathetic picture prevailed, and we were whisked ahead to the counter.

I could see the customers in line were already bleeding from their eyes because we had pulled the "helpless family" routine and jumped ahead. Things ratcheted up as we began to weigh our bags.

Jen had ignored my earlier request to weigh her gargantuan, oversized gorilla of a suitcase at home. I had even recently purchased a handheld luggage reader instead of having to balance it on the bathroom scale. As I tossed it up on the metal plate, I watched the digital readout with bated breath, like some off-Broadway version of roulette, hoping for a fifty. Fifty was the magic number we needed so that we didn't have to either pay an extra baggage fee (wife won't do it) or shed some weight. It came up sixty-two. Busted.

Instead of her getting it sorted out at home, now I needed to spring into action to open up all of our suitcases in the middle of the airport floor. I was responsible for dividing twelve pounds of slingshot underwear and blow-dryers equally among four different bags, shifting weight, trying to come in under fifty pounds to avoid paying a fee on top of a fee.

I converted my anger to determination and fixed my eyes to the floor, looked straight ahead, and prayed that no one in the line behind us made an attempt on our lives.

Airport policy required me to dump the Smarte Carte after check-in, but my load was lightened to our carry-on, two personal items, stroller, and dog-in-a-duffel. In an effort to maximize my efficiency, I chose my strategy.

I fixed a bag on my north, south, west, and east sides. Each bag had a shoulder strap that lassoed around my neck, including one with a dog in it. A bag in front, back, left, and right. I was starting to get some serious chafing on my neck but had to press on. It was almost like I had four seat belts simultaneously cutting into my delicate neck skin. I looked like the chair-o-planes ride at the carnival as I walked up to security.

As if the physical challenge at check-in wasn't enough, I now had to break everything down to go through the X-ray machine. The same people from downstairs whom I had jumped in front of in line were now stuck waiting behind me yet again going through the X-ray station as I undid my belt while standing next to our pyramid of belongings.

I pulled the laptops out, got the jewelry into the small dish, pulled the kid out of the car seat and tossed it up onto the belt. I folded up the stroller and took out the breast milk to be tested. As I took my shoes off and held my terrier under my arm, I shot a glance to the peanut gallery behind me, huffing, tapping their feet, and making fake coughing noises to encourage me to speed up.

Like I was enjoying having to do this. Instead of standing there like a bunch of momos, why not offer me some help?

But rest easy because it's all worth it after you shuffle through the metal detector in your socks, holding your pants up, watching your assembly line of shit stuffed in a dozen trays back up the conveyor belt.

If you're on time, a few airlines will still preboard families onto the flight. It allows folks like me to get on the airplane and get the family situated before a gaggle of impatient passengers backs up behind you. Unfortunately, by the time we got to the gate, they were already loading the final zone.

"Holy shit! This guy had better not sit next to me," was the look on most everyone's face. With Ava's satin swaths of fabric (known as "babies") Springsteening out of my back pockets, her suckers (pacifiers) on a chain around my neck, my doggie duffel and zebra-striped bottle warmer bag, I fought my way through twenty-eight rows. All the while, my bags were scraping people's arms and banging off their faces, triggering buried toys to come to life with annoying catch phrases and theme songs. I lobbed out "sorries" and "my bads" as I headed toward the rear of the plane.

Most of the overhead bins were already closed, a telltale sign that we were officially screwed. I walked up and down the middle aisle with everyone already seated, opening various bins, trying furiously to punch and jam our shit in. As I struggled, I saw an attendant approaching, thinking that he might be able to offer his help.

Instead, the jubilant member of the flight crew wearing a Santa hat asked me to hurry up, find somewhere to put my bags and take a seat. I finally found a spot, joined my wife in the back of the plane, and tucked Cooper under my seat.

A friend once told me that the best way to squash any passenger uprisings or physical attacks on you or your family was to liquor up everyone in the area. Free booze trumps screaming baby almost every time . . . that and a bag of ear plugs. I ended up having to buy only two beers, plus the four for myself, which ran me over thirty bucks because my neighbors drank imports.

One little thing I learned about flying with kids was that if you can manage to usurp everyone's preconceived idea of what they thought their flight was going to be by having a quiet baby, you'll be showered with praise upon exit.

"I didn't even know there was a baby on board. What a darling!" chimed in an old man.

"She's such a sweetheart. The first one is always the best, eh?" one woman quipped.

"You know, she really is a sweetheart. Sometimes I even forget I'm traveling with a ten-pound kid kick-starting my genitals in footie PJ's. Where the fuck were you with the kudos when we stepped on the plane four hours ago?" I wanted to say.

We were on the ground in Atlanta and working our way

toward a family bathroom in the terminal. The concept of a family bathroom was unique, and this was my first experience with one. It's a small room with a changing station, sink, and toilet, along with some alternative counter space to keep your bags off the floor.

Sometimes you'll get lucky with these, like no one's even used it before; other times you'll walk into a war zone of shredded toilet paper, maxi-pad wrappers, and blown-out Huggies left behind by the last family of savages before you.

We met my mother-in-law and father-in-law at the baggage carousel, their able bodies, helping us to avoid another Smarte Carte episode. As I opened my arms to embrace my in-laws with a hug, they swiftly floated right by, as if I were invisible. That's another thing I had to get used to. I'm not as cute as a newborn baby and never will be. We loaded up and headed toward their house, about an hour from the airport.

On the ride back, we were briefed on the schedule for the week. There was certainly no shortage of activities and opportunities to visit with different family members and introduce Ava to everyone.

The next day, we took her to the Lenox Square Mall to get her first picture taken with Santa.

I'm all about tradition and the holidays. It's one of the many things I love about Jen's family, how dedicated they are to celebrating the holidays.

I remember how important it was for my mom to take us (me and my two brothers) to get our pictures taken with Old St. Nick. I grew up in an extremely rural area about an hour outside of Philadelphia. Mom would send us outside ten minutes before we were supposed to leave. I was to start the car ahead of time to warm it up and supervise my brothers as we beat frozen chunks of ice and slush off the wheel wells of the vehicle with broomsticks. I couldn't believe that Mom had the patience to brave the snow and ice-covered roads simply to fulfill a tradition for us.

We drove to the closest mall, in Quakertown, Pennsylvania, a fairly undeveloped town at the time. Dad stayed behind to keep an eye on the woodstove. He wasn't one for malls; in fact, I'm not sure I've ever seen him remotely near one. As a kid, I got the impression that this event was some sort of hillbilly meet-up, with lots of farmers and country folk in overalls standing in line with their families.

At what point did this novelty wear off? Trading stories with other hayseeds, watching my brothers wrestle to the death over a Walkman on the dirty mall floor, my mom hanging on to our so-called tradition (and her sanity) by a thread.

Santa's aroma was that of some shitty, dried-out "Allentown Brown" weed. His belt buckle was plastic, and the fake beard peppered with coffee stains bordered on pathetic.

How did Mom think this was legit? The truth was, it didn't matter. It was tradition, and that's what was important.

I wondered how Ava's experience would differ from mine, some twenty-five years later. Not only were we going to see Santa, but my wife's family also has a tradition of riding Macy's miniature train, the Pink Pig. It's set up under a canopy on the top level of the parking structure and has been a fixture around those parts for decades during the holiday season.

The line for Santa was already a hundred people deep when we'd parked and walked inside to get our tickets for the Pig. I started to wonder whether or not an eight-week-old baby really needed to deliver her Christmas requests to the old man, considering she was just born and had about a thousand gifts at home that were still brand-new. But again, tradition.

We got in line and, as we rounded the corner, I caught a peek of Mr. Christmas.

Wow. Things have changed in twenty-five years. Ava got lucky. Santa didn't look at all like he slept off a bender in the backseat of a Chevelle. In fact, he donned a festive velour romper with silver buckles and shiny boots. He was well groomed, polite, and resembled a sexy Kenny Loggins. The wonderland around him was fluffy, pristine, and sparkling with holiday magic. Even I was considering hopping on the old man's lap for a spin. Hell, this might be good for my soul.

Ava didn't make a peep, and Santa held her perfectly. He assured her that she would have an unforgettable first Christmas and commented to Jen and me that we had a beautiful baby girl. What a charmer!

We moved along, past the beauty of his Christmas wonderland, to the part where his helpers try and upsell you into buying a three-hundred-picture press kit. We ordered our *one* photo (scan, e-mail as many as you want) and moved back upstairs to get in line (again) for the Pink Pig.

I was starting to get the hang of standing in line. Between the airport and the mall, I was a seasoned pro. After about an hour, we got to the front and my wife realized there was a height requirement, which restricted infants who couldn't sit up on their own from riding the train.

We were deflated and angry that this was ruining the start of our first Christmas tradition. Personally, I have a long way to go in dealing with things that don't work out perfectly. I'm kind of like a kid in that regard. I closed my eyes and pretended I was dancing in a meadow, pushing away the urge to blow past the train operator and derail this choo-choo with my fists.

After a few minutes, Jen returned from speaking with the manager. She must've done something right, because they allowed her to get right on the train with Ava. We propped her up like *Weekend at Bernie's*, and the train left the station. Probably not a stellar parenting move, but sometimes you just have to say screw it. Tradition sometimes trumps rational thinking.

With the two main events of the Atlanta holiday out of the way, all we had to worry about now was donating to Toys for Tots, going to see Rudolph at the Center for Puppetry Arts, having several meals around town with family, enduring the marathon gift session on Christmas day, and the men's annual two-day camping trip to the top of Mount Le Conte the day after Christmas.

Christmas morning was fun because Ava couldn't open anything on her own. Sure, we faked a gift or two, tearing the paper and throwing her in front of it for a photo opportunity, but for the most part my wife and I were on double duty.

I couldn't believe how many gifts she had, and in classic fashion, I started to get ahead of myself, knowing that since we were headed to Philadelphia after this, we'd have to ship everything to Los Angeles. My only hope was that Ava would get a few FedEx gift cards to ring in the season!

Two days after Christmas, we (me, father-in-law, uncle-in-law, and brother-in-law) embarked on our annual camping trip to the Great Smoky Mountains National Park. I wasn't sure if I should go this year, as I'd be leaving Jen all alone with Ava, who was only two months old. It made me feel a little selfish, but at the same time, I secretly wanted a break. I downplayed how important it was and asked Jen to be honest with me, and she encouraged me to go. So the next day, the four of us piled into Uncle Bill's car and made the four-hour journey north.

We entered the park in Gatlinburg, Tennessee, and drove to the trailhead where we normally park. From there, it's a seven-mile hike to the top of the mountain, where we would set up camp in an old three-sided Adirondack shelter.

It was out of cell phone range, which meant I would have two solid days of silence. No ringing, buzzing, or chirping of toys or phones, no crying or screaming—just nature and me. It sounded like heaven.

I put in a final phone call before we lost our signal and told my wife and Ava that I loved them (true) and would miss them (white lie). We unloaded the car, got our gear ready, and started the trek. The temperature on this particular trip happened to be minus four with gusts up to sixty miles per hour and whiteout snow squalls.

Once we reached the top, I began to wonder who might've made out better that weekend, Jen or myself. As the sun fell behind the horizon, we fired up our portable camping stoves and got down to the business of eating freeze-dried food and nipping whiskey.

At the end of the evening, just before we turned in, we sat in front of the shelter, talking in "dude." You know, wrenches and dry rubs, Sofía Vergara and which team would make it to the Super Bowl. As I switched to chamomile to warm the insides, I scanned the perimeter with my headlamp and noticed several sets of eyes just beyond the reach of my light. We were being stalked by a pack of wolves.

After about a half an hour, we had cleaned up our stoves and excess food and hoisted them high above the ground on cables in an effort to keep them away from the wolves, but even more so, the local bear community.

Evidently this worked, and our friends disappeared. I lay on my back, listening to the wind blast over the top of the mountain with a hand warmer shoved in my underwear. The cold air had killed my iPod battery, and my snot was slowly starting to freeze to my face. I realized to exactly what lengths I would go to find a little time to myself. I just didn't know if it was worth it.

We drove back to Atlanta, and the next day, I packed up the toy haul into four boxes, took it to FedEx, and boarded the plane for the second leg of our trip, headed to my parents' house in Philadelphia.

HELLO GOOD-BYE

The weather along the entire Eastern Seaboard was disgusting, with wind chills around zero, blustery and snowy.

We went through the paces, just like before, to check in and board the plane. Fortunately, we had planned a little better this time (weighed our bags) and were in time to get loaded on the plane early.

The flight was quick, which was a good thing. The plane we were on felt like someone had sewn wings onto an old school bus. The heat was barely working, and as we made our descent into Philadelphia, we were battered and beaten by the crosswinds. My ass had come off the seat more than once, same with Jen. This can be nerve-racking enough when you're by yourself, but try it while hanging on to an infant. It gives a whole new meaning to bouncing the baby. We were in a martini shaker with 130 other people, and the atmosphere was tense.

It was safe to say that we didn't have "Sully" Sullenberger at the helm on this one, but thankfully the pilot did manage to straighten us out just in time for the wheels to hit the tarmac.

My dad picked us up at the airport and was excited to see his granddaughter. It had been only two months since he was in L.A. for the birth, but I'm sure that felt like forever.

It took us about an hour to get to my parents' house. It was Ava's first time on the Pennsylvania Turnpike (scratch that off her bucket list) and her first time seeing snow. I'm sure she'll remember one of those things over the other . . . and I'm not talking about the overpriced two-lane toll road.

As we pulled up the driveway, it was a Norman Rockwell moment with snow hanging on the boughs of the trees and candles in each of the windows. My parents spent some time trading Ava back and forth, Cooper found his spot in front of the fire, and my mom and Jen gave Ava a bath before dinner.

We loaded up my mom's car and headed down to the Spinnerstown Hotel for a bite to eat. Jen was a bit nervous about me driving on black ice, but I reassured her that just because I'd lived on Venice Beach for the last few years, didn't mean that I'd forgotten how.

Most of the restaurants in the country are old hotels, converted into pubs and bar/restaurants. The bar was packed with holiday partiers, so we decided to stay classy and grab a seat in the restaurant. Something told me that the drunk roofers at the bar probably weren't going to smash out their Marlboro Reds just because my kid was there. We downed some Yuengling Lagers and church-made pierogies and made it back to my mom and dad's house unscathed.

Ava slept in her Pack 'n Play in front of my dad's bird-watching window as the woodstove crackled in the background. We had more beer in frosted mugs and watched the end of *Christmas Vacation*. The holidays just wouldn't be the same without Cousin Eddie standing in the street telling Clark that his shitter was full. So maybe it was one part Norman Rockwell, one part Al Bundy, but it was all parts great.

It snowed again overnight, and we decided to let my parents have some fun with Ava (code for us sleeping in) while we ate breakfast in bed. After eating, we watched my dad snowblow the driveway and chop up firewood for the stove.

We got Ava dressed so she could see my middle brother, her uncle Eric. He had been unable to make it to Los Angeles for the birth, so we were excited for him to see Ava for the first time.

As I handed her to him, I could see a bit of discomfort on his face. He could tell me all day long that he knew what he was doing when he went to hold a baby, but I could clearly see he might need a pointer or two.

A high school football standout, Eric was always good at tucking the football under his arm, so I went with that analogy. After a few minutes, the awkwardness dissipated, and I could see on his face that he was truly in awe of the situation and how amazing it really was.

He took a seat and helped her unwrap the Christmas present he'd brought. It's been a running joke for several years now, but Eric's gift-wrapping approach has always been a little lackluster. The heart and sentiment were there, but he fell short with the execution. This time, the wrapping paper around the present was held together with black electrical tape, which looked like he pulled and stretched or maybe even chewed his way to end the roll.

Nonetheless, I was glad to see the excitement in my family's eyes as they played and cuddled with their first grandchild and niece.

With the days being shorter, we decided to hop in the car before it got dark and take a drive down to my grandfather's house.

Grandpop had led a very full life. He'd been a high school football star, served in the army toward the end of WWII, had five kids, and had served as a police officer, a county detective, and a district judge.

He had been diagnosed with peripheral vascular disease, which resulted in the eventual amputation of his left leg, leaving him confined to a wheelchair in his house. My dad had built ramps around the property for him, so he could access different rooms and do simple tasks like get outside to get the mail. A man who'd once had the ability to control people's lives and fates in a court of law was now struggling to maintain control for himself.

As we sat in his living room and he held Ava, I couldn't help but think about how few people actually get to meet their great-grandparents. My mom coordinated a picture of us (Ava, me, my dad, and his dad) all together.

In the car, after we left, I stared at the picture on my phone, looking at four generations of my family. I was so happy that we had decided to go and see him that day because that visit turned out to be Ava's first and last.

A few months later, my grandfather died. It was the only time that Ava ever got to meet him. I know he'll be looking down on us as we grow old, and I'll be sure to show her the picture and tell her about the day she got to meet him in person, even though she won't remember.

In the hustle and bustle of everyday life, we often take our family for granted. We tell ourselves that we're too busy to stop by or get together and that we'll do it next week, or next year; no big deal. Sometimes there is no next week. Experiencing life and death within such a short period of time gave me some much-needed perspective. Life is precious and I didn't have time to become complacent.

The next day, we packed up our stuff once again and headed to the airport. Destination: Los Angeles.

CHAPTER 4

Sahd State of Affairs

LOST AND NOT FOUND

My lips were chapped, my face was windburned, and my neck had rope burn from the airport duffel bags. Collectively, we had been through the wringer. Three flights and three weeks on the road with a newborn and a dog had taken its toll. It was fantastic to see both families, to be able to introduce Ava to our extended families and establish a tradition. BUT HOLY HELL.

I was anxious to get back to work. I had already developed and sold a few pilots and series to the E! network and was excited to return to the atmosphere of the late-night show *Chelsea Lately*. Even though I didn't technically work for that show, my office was next to theirs, with my focus being on other projects to expand Chelsea Handler's brand.

I had plans to move into some scripted properties, which were what I knew best from my days of working for Happy

Madison. My contract was up in May, and I was anxious to prove my worth so they'd want to renew and keep me around.

The bottom line was that for twelve years I'd been working in entertainment, specifically in comedy, and I loved it. Who could ask for anything more than to be able to go to work in a T-shirt and sneakers and write dick and fart jokes all day?

It was the first week of January, the beginning of a new year, and I was back in my office. I was catching up on e-mails and phone calls, riding high on being a new dad and excited about my great job. Every symbol on the slot machine was coming up WINNER.

Within a few hours, I had a meeting with one of the partners. What I thought the meeting was going to be and how it turned out were at opposite ends of the spectrum. It was supposed to be a "state of the union" upon entering the new year.

There were downsizing their development department, eliminating my position and weren't going to be able to bring me back in May. I was under contract for the next few months, but they emphasized that I should go and spend some time with my new family and use that time to find my next endeavor. As he left my office, I sat alone in an uncomfortable silence.

The economy was in the midst of tanking, and we were entering a recession. I'd just had a baby and bought a new car. Ava was enrolled in a pricey day care. I was short of breath. The room started spinning, and I thought I might black out. Before everything went dark and I woke up with my face tattooed to the carpet, I took a few deep breaths and steadied myself.

I needed to focus on the positive. Thankfully, my wife

was starting back at work, which was a huge step up from the last few weeks of maternity "disability" pay.

I took a long lunch and came back toward the end of the day to start boxing up stuff and taking down the framed mementos that hung on my walls. The Jim Carrey poster from the days when he still did stand-up, pictures of me and Louis Anderson, Drew Carey, Sandler, and others.

Framed comedy album covers with credits that went out of their way to thank me for helping them along the way. Pictures backstage at comedy clubs and thank-yous from the guys I had put on national late-night TV for the first time.

I waited until everyone had gone for the day before I wheeled yet another maintenance cart to the elevator and loaded up my car, trying to avoid any awkward explanations.

As I drove west on Interstate 10 toward the beach, with the sun in my eyes, reality set in quickly. I was out of a job. I was no longer a breadwinner. I pulled off and turned down Navy Street in Venice to the dead end that overlooked the beach.

I stared out at the water and counted the waves in each set for about an hour, trying to keep my mind from telling my body to commit to a panic attack. I gazed out the window like Bill Paxton in *Apollo 13*, hoping that I wouldn't burn up in the reentry process and would live to see another day.

I had just spent the last twelve years as an executive with all the perks. No more rides on the private jet, private chefs, premieres, paid business trips, or expense accounts.

That night, Jen and I weighed our options and talked about how we would adapt and adjust to the new circumstances. I thought maybe I would take some time to clear my head, let day care handle Ava while I fully focused on my next career move, but then . . .

JEN: You're not thinking we're gonna keep her in day care every day while you play *Call of Duty* and have lunch beers, are you?

ME: It's not like I'm on vacation, Jen. I'll meet people for coffee and stuff . . . plus put my feelers out there. If she's at day care, it leaves me open to make an interview at any time without complication.

JEN: Well, what about your downtime? You can't expect a dozen interviews right off the bat. Maybe you could take my jeans to get hemmed and repaint Ava's nursery to finally match the bedding. Or even better, meet with the accountant and get our taxes done early!

ME: Uhh . . . *No.* Maybe you're onto something here. Maybe I can watch her and still manage my job search.

JEN: I think you can manage a job search and watching Ava at the same time. If you have an interview come up, we'll find a sitter. I'm sorry, babe. I love you. But you've got to be realistic.

The very next day, I started my new gig. Taking care of a twelve-week-old baby girl.

STEP INTO MY OFFICE,
DON'T MIND THE TOILET

The poor alarm clock didn't even have a chance to do its job. Ava was up at five thirty a.m., and Jen was getting ready for work after almost sixteen weeks of being at home, bonding.

Luckily for us, she had a great job, also in television. She had given me the tour of everything that she used during the day, gave me a ballpark idea of what Ava's schedule was and what to do if I couldn't get her to stop crying or if she crapped out of her onesie.

All of a sudden, I wished I had paid more attention to what was going on the last six weeks we were together at home.

I mustered up some temporary confidence and reassured her that everything was going to be fine and she shouldn't worry, to focus on enjoying her first day back at work after being out for four months. As she kissed us and pulled the door closed behind her, it got quiet. Ava and I sat there for a few minutes staring at each other.

Okay. Now what? What time does your mom get home? Oh. Right. She just left. Maybe I should do something to take my mind off the obvious, feeling sorry for myself and wondering what in the hell my next move was.

Everything that had been removed from my man cave was now sitting in Tupperware tubs in the dining room, former home of the baby shower gift pyramid. The pile was significantly larger now that I had added everything from my office to it.

Without the cave or an office, I needed to stake claim somewhere, anywhere. Now that the home was my new workplace, I needed to find a place to plant my flag.

It took only a few minutes before the epiphany. I owned one remaining piece of real estate in our apartment. She had *her* bathroom and I had *my* bathroom. I pitched the idea to Ava and spent the afternoon devising a plan.

These were the playoffs and without a win, my season would be over. It was the bottom of the ninth with two outs . . . and that night we went to dinner to celebrate Jen's first day back. I stepped up to the dish to rally an offensive and pitch my wife the idea of changing the theme in my bathroom.

I spit into my batting gloves and rubbed them together, took a few practice swings, and did what any real man would do.

ME: You know . . . since we've been married, I've pretty much let you run the show with our decor and I've really made a concerted effort to compromise on these decisions.

JEN (with a smirk): Go ahead. You can start decorating if you want. What do you have in mind? Are you gonna hang another beer sign over the bed like your old apartment when we were dating? Or maybe use your college T-shirt quilt instead of the duvet?

ME: No, yeah, I get it. I'm definitely no interior design maven. What I'm trying to say is . . . that I really like what you've done in my bathroom with the jasmine soaps and the dead sticks in a vase. I even think the folded hand towels are cute, but . . .

Jen's facial expressions were quickly on the defensive, and I could sense some immediate opposition to whatever I was going to say. I jumped out of the batter's box, choked up on my bat, and went with "Plan B," an overly dramatic confession playing to her soft side.

ME: Look. I've lost my job. The e-mails have stopped, my phone doesn't ring anymore, and I'm slipping into irrelevancy. My pride is shattered and self-worth is barely existent. I've boxed up my manhood, destined for storage, and I'm going to be spending eleven hours a day with a two-month-old girl who can't talk to me. I just want to hang on to a few important things from my old space. I'll put them in my bathroom, so I can have a moment every now and again to remember where I've come from . . . that's all.

JEN: Hasn't it been only one day at home alone with Ava?

ME: Timelines are irrelevant, Jen. I'm dying a slow death over here.

Jen was silent. Whether she believed me or threw in the towel on this conversation, the plan worked. It wasn't eloquent or pretty, but it worked. I had hit a home run. Forget about the corked bat that was my Oscar award–winning sob story. My performance didn't get us tossed from the restaurant before the food was served, and I now had a place to hang my hat. I rounded the bases, pointing my index finger to the heavens as my teammates mobbed me in front of the dugout.

I kept the valuable PEZ dispensers (without the feet), the original 1980s G.I. Joes, LEGO Minifigures, five hundred wine corks (because, seriously guys, I am going to make that corkboard someday), some vintage signs, and miscellaneous important figurines.

I operated my cluttered nine-by-nine toy-filled bathroom like a museum, and access was now strictly monitored. It was a fragile microcosm with twenty-four-hour climate control. In an effort to avoid sweat-bending any of the figurine packaging, I'd committed to taking brief, cold showers to eliminate the potential for any steam damage.

It was a small price to pay to be surrounded by my old friends. I did most of my thinking (hiding) in there and will admit that I could really cozy up, sitting on the plastic toilet seat lid, feathering through a recent copy of *Beckett's Baseball Card Price Guide* in silence. Sure, I had to stand on the side of

the tub and reach into the corner of the ceiling for a cell signal to refresh my Web browser, but no big deal.

Once I closed the door and turned the lock, it was a full-
on Calgon moment. Take me away, brother. Take me away.

As soon as Jen was home from work, I dove in (tried not
to hit my head on the toilet) and reminisced with my old
keepsakes. I enjoyed the peace. I even silenced the room of
external noise by toweling up the bottom of the door, an old
college trick to keep the weed smoke from reaching the hallway sprinklers in the dorm.

From here on out, any important calls or meetings would
take place in my new office, the quietest and calmest room in
the house. I even put the name placard from my desk right
there on the vanity, next to my toothbrush holder.

So if you want to take a meeting or just hang for a bit,
leave a message with my assistant (voice mail) and we'll set
something up.

CHAIRMAN OF THE BORED

With Jen gone every day at work, Ava and I fell into a pretty basic routine. She was really just a blob. She could barely sit up, so crawling or even rolling over were out of the question.

All I had to do was move our four-month-old from one station to the next so she didn't get bedsores. Twenty minutes in the doorjamb swing, another ten in the bouncer, and finish her off with some tummy time. I had this thing licked.

The idea of going outside seemed monumental, and there were just too many variables. I lacked self-confidence and couldn't bear the thought of being in a position where I'd have to deal with any type of emergency in public.

I had a recurring nightmare about being in Bloomingdale's without diapers or wipes, a baby who had just deployed a wicked diaper loaf strapped to my chest, and having to retreat to a changing room while patrons fell to their knees, choking and gasping for air.

Let's be honest. That *could* happen, and I just didn't have the inner strength, knowledge, or patience to deal with it. While Ava endured my version of infant circuit training, I got acquainted with how heinous daytime TV was. How did anyone survive watching this shit? (ABC Daytime—you need a TV development exec to revamp your programming? Gimme a jingle!)

I gave up on the local stations. When I wasn't sucked into the *The Dark Knight* on HBO for the umpteenth time, I took on the task of relieving some of the pressure on the DVR, purging it of everything my wife deemed as "shit you can watch by yourself." My ass created a valley in the sofa and I developed blisters on my thumbs from playing Xbox.

Ava obviously wasn't talking, and without anyone else around to engage in conversation, I was forced to offer her my commentary as we watched old Westerns, survival shows, and *The Three Stooges*.

The neighbors passing by the balcony window could've assumed I was a mental patient, pacing around the living room in my work uniform (my bathing suit and T-shirt), barking about this and that.

I ranted about the differences between how Curly and Shemp delivered the paintbrush slap and paused *The Price Is Right* and used Google to cheat and win the Showcase Showdown. I also caught 162 baseball games that season, no modest feat.

I began to master my Baby Björn skills, making trips to the mailbox and eventually graduating to light housekeeping and cooking dinner. Ava had a blast just hanging out on my chest while I vacuumed.

So long as I kept her from banging her head as I rounded corners and her feet away from the cutting board while I prepped veggies and didn't burn her toesies on the inside of the oven door, I was golden. I filled in the grooves of the day with a few milk bottles (her) and a couple of power naps (me). Before I knew it, my wife was home from work.

Having created a comfort zone at our apartment was fantastic, but the downside was that I had become a recluse. At six weeks in, I started to resemble an albino version of Gollum from *The Lord of the Rings*. A subtle spare tire was advancing on my waistline, and my muscles weren't far from a state of atrophy.

I knew that I needed a plan. I had to leave the apartment at least once a day to maintain some form of sanity. I decided to break the ice with a walk down to the beach. It was only two blocks away, and I was a grown man; what could happen that I wouldn't be able to handle?

I covered our pale bodies in an armor of SPF 50 and outfitted the jogging stroller with all the bells and whistles. I had my phone fully charged, milk for her, and a snack for me.

I set Ava up with two suckers and tucked a "baby" in along her side with a wooden HABA toy or two. In our household, a "baby" was a satin patch of cloth made by a company named Swaddle Designs. We deemed them "babies." They were always there to comfort her, whether she was crying or having trouble falling asleep.

I cued up Tom Petty's "Into the Great Wide Open" on my iPhone and dropped it into the cup holder, and we were ready to rock. As we stepped outside, the sun hit us like water on the wicked witch. I pulled the sun cover over Ava's head and dropped my Ray-Bans from my forehead into position. We made it across the street and up and over the windy path leading down to the beach.

I gained confidence with every step. A house wasn't going to fall on us, and strangers weren't pointing and laughing because I wasn't at work. We saw girls in bikinis Rollerblading and playing volleyball and people out for an afternoon walk. I passed another guy pushing a kid in a stroller, and we apprehensively gave each other the "Jeep wave" (Jeep owners always wave to each other in passing on the road) and nodded with a smile.

That wave said a lot. It said, "I feel your pain, brother, and you're not alone." I realized that fun and exciting things were happening every day while I Poltergeisted in front of the TV like Heather O'Rourke.

Who was I to deny Ava fun and fresh air? Life was moving on without us.

I pushed the stroller and daydreamed, watching the waves crash and girls in bikinis jump up and down on the sand. I felt the ocean breeze against my skin and got distracted. I hadn't been doing a great job of paying attention to my immediate surroundings.

After we came down the path from the esplanade and were well onto the beach strand, I bent down to check in on Ava.

Everything was gone but the kid. Baby, sucker, toys. All gone. What in the hell had happened? Had someone mugged my baby while I was daydreaming, or had she picked this particular moment in time to learn how to start throwing stuff?

Jen had put a higher value on these pieces of cloth than most of the stuff we owned. This would be almost as bad as if

I had lost the girl. I was yanked out of lollygag dreamland and into a straight-up panic.

I had just descended a few hundred yards down the beach and had to do an about-face. I wasn't just jogging with this stroller. I was pumping my legs back up the hill like I was trying out for the Olympic team.

How long ago and how far back had she dropped these? My only hope was that in the eight minutes since I'd lost these things, a bum hadn't picked up the baby and used it as a dinner napkin or to clean his ass.

Then I saw something in the distance. It was one of the wooden toys. I backtracked to the top of the hill and found everything right there in a pretty little line. She must've just dropped everything.

This simple walk had not only made my thighs numb, but made me feel better. Sure, most of the walk was spent in a seized-up panic with an elevated heart rate, but there were at least three or four minutes of pure breathtaking beauty and relaxation. I felt invigorated and sensed the signs of a renewed confidence about being able to survive on my own, with Ava, outside of the living room.

I began to accept my unexpected situation as some sort of twisted blessing, knowing that the time I was spending with my daughter now was time that I would never get back.

I was no longer chairman of the bored.

THE BATTLE OF GROCERY HILL

A few weeks later, I was still riding high on my trip out of the house and noticed we were getting low on supplies. A trip to the grocery store was breathing down my neck, and no longer did I feel the need to wait until Saturday when Jen and I could go together.

I needed to prove to myself that I could be self-sufficient and evolve into this new role as a stay-at-home dad. As I watched Ava yell at me from her Pack 'n Play while I constructed a ketchup sandwich for lunch, I decided that enough was enough.

I rolled up my sleeves and told myself I would put an end to the living room loitering and focus on a solid plan of attack. I would treat this like it was a mission. The grocery store was our frenemy, and we needed to conquer it because, quite frankly, we were out of toilet paper *and* baby wipes (my personal backup before paper towels), and the situation was dire. I threw my diaper bag on the floor and started filling it with everything I would need for this special op.

The pack I chose for this mission (unfortunately) resembled a Euro man-purse, a sort of dainty over-the-shoulder messenger bag, but the fact that it was camouflage gave me built-in street cred. It was outfitted with several pockets for which I could separate my tools arsenal.

The goal was to travel light and float free like a butterfly, able to dance from branch to branch above my enemies' heads as I moved in for the kill (item purchase). Clearly, I had forgotten my goal as I stuffed at least twenty diapers and a few washcloths in my bag for an hour-long excursion to the market.

One plastic bag filled with yogurt melts, another with cheddar goldfish. I was prepared for both types of cravings, sweet *and* savory. I brought several toys, double-checking that none of them made noise. We were going "guns off," no batteries included. I didn't need to give away my location in the field with a toy that could at any moment begin blaring "Row, Row, Row Your Boat" from the depths of my Euro murse.

I strapped on my Similac grenades, one warm, another cold. A "baby" as a bandanna and three pacifiers attached to a necklace like dog tags.

I buttoned up our bag, threw it over my shoulder, and came to the abrupt realization that it weighed more than my kid. This certainly wasn't stealth and instead of a day pack, it looked like I was hiking the Pacific Crest for two months.

I stood there facing myself in the mirror and felt absolutely ridiculous. What was I doing? I needed to thin this bag out before I slipped a disk.

Instead of using the Baby Bjorn, I decided to keep Ava in the car seat, which slid out of the car and conveniently popped into the ultralight Snap N Go stroller. It was quick and agile, exactly what I needed. I rolled the windows up, closed the moonroof and dropped the sunshades on the back windows. We slowed our roll and pumped lullabies by Metallica as we made a dry run through the parking lot and surveyed our point of entry.

I served two tours of my own as a teenager, stocking shelves at a Weis Market through the night, and had mastered store setups. I knew about the weather conditions in the freezer aisle and how to maneuver past the bouncy ball cage without setting them all free. I had the knowledge and tools to complete this objective.

If I stayed focused and followed my plan, nothing could go wrong. Ava had already eaten plenty of food, and I gave her ample time to digest but not digest enough that we might encounter a rear blowout while shopping. At the very worst, I might have to negotiate changing a soggy one in public, but I would rise to the challenge.

I checked my watch, closed my eyes, and collected myself for a moment. It was go time. We hit the ground hard and fast. I pulled the car seat out, dropped it into the stroller, and moved away from the convoy as we mobilized toward the cart corral, camo bag and bushel of recycled grocery bags in tow. As we approached the rally point, I started to waver, wondering if maybe I should've opted for the Björn instead.

Our first snag was the antiseptic Clorox wipe station for the carts. No surprise that it was empty. I was supposed to be a warrior, but let's be honest, I couldn't afford to catch a cold. I wrestled with the lid of the container and poured the remaining juices onto the handle of our cart. With the threat of contamination eliminated, we turned toward the door and stared down our next objective.

Wait a second. How in the hell was I going to push a stroller *and* a cart at the same time? Clearly I was having a logistical brainfart. My goal to enter the store like an assassin came off looking more like I was doing a drunk shuffle to the *Benny Hill* theme song. I hee-hawed back and forth, trying to get the stroller and the cart through the automatic sliding glass doors. They banged back and forth, making violent jerking motions, causing Ava to cry, while I stood in between them getting blasted by the artificial wind blower used to keep houseflies out of the store. I had just won the asshole award.

However, I wasn't raised a quitter. I was always told to get up after you got knocked down. Perseverance inspired me to drag both the stroller and cart across the front of the store.

At first I tried the two-arm power push, stroller in one arm, cart in the other. Unfortunately I didn't have a shopping lane fifteen feet wide. The deli line forced me to move single-file, which ended with me banging my shins and heels off the fronts and backs of the carts.

My tactic lacked serious efficiency, and I fell back to the car to ditch the stroller and go mobile. The Baby Björn would offer me the flexibility that I needed. I loaded the stroller into the car and spent a few minutes bending and twirling my arms through the Björn straps while referencing the instructions.

After I concluded my whirling dervish in the parking lot, I made my way back inside, beyond the deli. I waded through the imaginary trails that connected the cheese islands to the muffin displays and paused at the bakery to reload. I made Ava hug a loaf of French bread (it was on the list) and I grabbed one, too, and we held them like RPGs and strafed our way into produce making fake launch noises.

The adrenaline rush kicked in, and we were finally in command. The Rolling Stones' "Paint It Black" was the sound track in my head and, so far, no sign of enemy insurgents: diarrhea and vomiting. So far, so good.

The Bjorn was my new key to winning this battle. I danced through fruits and vegetables with unencumbered motions like I was auditioning for *South Pacific*.

I paused our cart briefly to engage in hand-to-hand combat with some plastic produce bags. At the same time, a middle-aged woman had approached—a field nurse perhaps—and bent over in front of us to pick out some eggplant. She wore classic khaki cuffed mom shorts, pulled up six to eight inches too high, with a tucked-in polo shirt and gold hoop earrings as big as doughnuts. She was part of the coalition and, unfortunately, was about to be on the receiving end of some friendly fire.

As I wrestled the bags from the dispenser, Ava fired off a double karate leg kick from her hanging position in the Bjorn, sending our cart shooting forward into the rear end of this poor woman. I stood in shock as she stumbled forward and masked her considerable pain while I fought to contain a burst of laughter brewing within.

I offered a halfhearted apology as she walked away, but I noticed a hint of irritation. I turned my head down and whispered into Ava's ear, "Next time, hold your fire, Private." She looked up at me as if she didn't have a clue what I was talking about and then swatted her hand at my face.

We trudged on, and Ava suddenly became animated. She was thrusting her feet back and forth uncontrollably, from my bladder to the bins of vegetables, connecting with a pyramid of avocados.

As several toppled to the floor, I danced backward like someone was shooting at my feet in an old Western. I bobbed my head left and right to see around the baby that was mounted to my chest. I went in and out of a birth squat to retrieve all the avocados.

We pushed on and flanked a wall of eggs from the left, holding my right finger in the air while making funny noises in an effort to distract Ava and secure a dozen brown eggs without making a floor omelet. As I pulled away, I noticed something out of my periphery.

An old lady was advancing on us, waving her cane and mumbling incoherently. Mind you, senior citizens are a national treasure, and they deserve all of our love and respect, but I knew what was coming.

This nana had us in her crosshairs and was closing in fast. She accelerated straight toward us in a designer sweat suit, arthritic fingers waving in front of her like a zombie from *Night of the Living Dead*. I could smell the scent of Elizabeth Arden perfume from twenty yards away.

We barely stood a chance. I didn't take my eyes off of her and frantically grabbed for anything besides Ava that I could use as a weapon. A hard salami, a soup can to the face, anything I could throw in her path.

It was too late. She was closing in fast and was now within a few feet. I motioned to Ava to fix bayonets as we shifted to close-quarters combat. I wasn't going to let this mummified artifact pinch the cheeks of my little soldier of (mis)fortune.

As she lunged at us, I juked left and straight-armed her off my body with a homegrown move I like to call the Elderly Heisman. I dazed and confused the old maid, and as she spun around, I heard her mumble in a rickety rocking-chair voice, "Come here and let me see her." We didn't have time to smoke unfiltered Camels and trade intelligence with this woman, so I left her behind for the next wave of stay-at-home parents to contend with. We needed to push through to our final mission objective, the cash register.

We were running out of daylight and kicked it into a higher gear. Ava was consumed by all of the pretty reds and pinks as we moved through beef and veal, but I kept her moving in and out of the aisles to avoid a screaming fit. I could sense that I needed to get her to the final rally point and into the infirmary for a nap.

Her vitals were weakening. With her arms and legs flailing, I high-stepped my way down the exact center of the aisle, keeping her appendages safely away from the glass condiment jars on the left and the spaghetti sauce on the right. I couldn't handle anything that may have cost me something under the "you break it, you buy it" policy.

I forged past floral to the cash register under covering fire (not really) and dove into an open lane, only to be met by some bleeding heart who wanted to play hero and help the struggling father unload his groceries onto the conveyor belt. Just when I thought I was in the clear, this double agent was inserting himself into my mission on the homestretch.

This guy hadn't sat with me in the war room while I planned this op. He didn't know my procedures for bagging. He didn't know that I wanted to put stuff up on the belt like I wanted it bagged. Today's baggers will throw your bleach in with your lunch meat and spit in your face on the way out. I'm wise to them and am always prepared with a counteraction.

I grouped my items on the belt a certain way—canned goods first, cold items together, and produce last. This ensures nothing is crushed as I drag the groceries to the Humvee. Plus, I was going for bragging rights. The less help, the better this story would be later.

Instead of going into a long, drawn-out explanation of my compulsive disorder, I told him Ava had pink-eye (not true, but a genius move) and that he'd be wise to take a step back.

He surrendered my cauliflower, and we passed through without incident. Our ride out of here was just beyond the bagger.

When prompted to enter my club number, Ava saw it as an opportunity to kick the debit-credit machine off its mount, just to let everyone know that we still had some fight left in us.

Brimming with confidence, I grabbed the receipt with my teeth and walked out of the explosions and carnage like John Rambo. Instead of a sweaty dude with an M60 machine gun under my arm, I held four recycled grocery bags and a blue-eyed baby girl strapped to my chest.

The only casualty on this mission was a box of melted Popsicles. Aside from that, no one died, and no one came home covered in shit or arrested. This was a successful campaign.

We arrived home only to be faced with our next mission: cleaning up the carnage I had left behind earlier that morning. I wanted to ignore it, but maintaining the household was now part of my daily gig.

HAZEL THE MAID

When I was a kid, on Saturday mornings while my dad did yard work, my mom would go grocery shopping and my brothers and I would stay behind to make pancakes, watch *Super Friends*, and annihilate the house.

We built bedsheet forts in the living room that made their way through the kitchen and into the den. We suspended the sheets from the tops of end tables and planters, the TV, and even the woodstove. We weighted down the corners with antique lamps and telephone books and constructed corridors underneath the sheets with sofa cushions and pillows.

The expansive linen-roofed estate had a back entrance that led up the stairs to our bedrooms. This was our main supply line/route to get plastic guns and swords distributed throughout the fort, so we could battle the shit out of one another.

It was only a matter of time before we could hear Mom's station wagon pulling up the driveway with an accompaniment of car doors opening and closing. She struggled up the path toward the front door, her arms clutching a slew of grocery bags. She was definitely wondering why we weren't out there to help (after honking the horn several times). The front door flew open and unbeknownst to her, it clipped the corner of our main sheet and triggered a total domino effect fort demolition.

Three rooms of connected sheets collapsed on our heads, leaving a few pint-sized ghostly protrusions sticking up in different rooms, yelling back and forth, trying to determine which asshole destroyed hours of our hard work. As we fought our way to daylight, Mom set the bags down on the kitchen table, turned to us, sitting amid the entire emptied linen closet, broken lampshades, and an armament of plastic weapons and simply said:

"There are more bags in the car. And you're out of your minds if you think I'm cleaning this up. Who do I look like, Hazel the maid?"

As we hauled the remaining grocery bags up the front lawn, my younger brothers asked me who Hazel was and why Mom was constantly overusing the reference. At the time, we had a great-aunt Hazel, but it couldn't have been her. She was a teacher, not a maid. I just didn't have the answers.

Years later, in college, with the help of syndication, Google, and drinking beer into the early mornings, I came to realize whom she was referring to all those years. Hazel was the star of a television sitcom in the sixties. She was a competent, take-charge, live-in maid. She toasted marshmallows with the Baxter family in their living room and baked homemade cookies while hustling around in a classic maid outfit complete with feather duster.

My generation had Tony Danza making it look like a snap, flexing a tricep workout while vacuuming the curtains, in between flipping pancakes and boxing in the garage. He dressed the kids and got them ready for bed in time to have a glass of wine with Mona in front of the fireplace.

Sitcom history has allowed me to believe that being a maid or a housekeeper is a pretty swank job.

As a newly minted SAHD, part of my duties probably fall within that territory. I cook, clean, and manage a household much like these stereotypical archetypes that preceded me . . . but I feel like maybe they missed a few important episodes.

Which sitcom showcased either of the maids catching a heel of their sneaker on some dog shit in the front yard and power-sliding their forehead into the car while buckling a car seat? Or the back spasms associated with bending down every five minutes to pick up a dropped toy?

How about the episode where the large Diet Coke gets pulled onto their lap at dinner? I don't recall ever seeing Hazel combing dried formula out of her beehive or soaking pieces of the breast pump in a tub of vinegar on a Friday night. And did Tony ever have to take a piss in a public bathroom with his daughter's feet dangling in a Baby Björn, threatening to interfere with his stream? I don't think I caught that episode.

And what about where they had to deal with explosive diarrhea that escaped from a diaper in the middle of a packed Anaheim convention center? Or realizing, after a near mental breakdown, that it's almost impossible to fold onesies and you should've been balling them up from the start.

Remember the one where five hundred Cheerios spilled out onto the equipment and floor at the eye doctor? Me neither. The endless hours spent correcting strangers about whether or not your kid is a boy or a girl? And that time that Angela asked Tony to return a shit-covered Diaper Genie to Babies "R" Us just because "they take everything back"? I didn't think so.

Times have definitely changed since Hazel's matching tiara and dusting apron and Tony's perfect pancakes. We've seen the good. Maybe it's about time to see what it's really like, for someone to show us some of the bad and the ugly.

CHAPTER 5

Out and About

I DREAM OF DIAPER GENIE

Once I had proven myself (to me *and* my wife), regular errands became my thing. I had to continue to get out of the house at least once a day or by late afternoon I'd want to kill myself.

Somewhere along the way, I got frustrated one night while trying to dispose of a loaded diaper in a Diaper Genie filled to capacity. It wasn't optimal timing, as I had left Ava on the bed and run twenty feet to the bathroom, all the while keeping an eye on her in the event she started to roll, which she did, immediately.

Instead of running back to grab her and making a more patient second attempt, I stomped my foot on the Genie pedal like I was trying to win Daytona and punched a shitty diaper through the already full receptacle. Needless to say, my impatience resulted in a set of broken "diaper jaws," as well as wet feces that was forced out of the diaper all over the wall and my T-shirt.

My wife had "implied" that it was my responsibility to return the item for a new one, since I was the one who had acted like an "impatient freak" and destroyed it. What am I going to tell the guy at customer service?

ME: I've got a broken Diaper Genie here.

EMPLOYEE: What happened?

ME: Good question, man. This thing just sucks. Poor craftsmanship. Probably made in China.

EMPLOYEE: So . . . you want to exchange it . . . for the same one?

ME: Sure.

Jen insisted that Babies "R" Us takes *anything* back, no questions asked.

I took her word for it and tossed it in the back of the family truckster and headed to the store. Ava and I were starting to find our groove and have some fun on our daily outings.

After Ava was born, aside from an occasional lullaby, I'd never really changed the music I listened to at all. I'm a white guy from farm country, so you've probably already guessed that I was a fan of hip-hop. Turned out, Ava and I both loved Jay-Z. The sweet beats of Hov kept our morning trips exciting.

We pulled into the parking lot, and I looked for one of

those golden spots that my dad always uses for his new truck. An isolated group of spots, toward the back of the parking lot in no-man's-land, would avoid door dings and runaway carts.

At first I couldn't tell if it was the fecal Genie in the back of the car that smelled so bad or if Ava had a fresh loaf from the buttocks bakery. Unfortunately, it was the latter. She'd waited until we left the house and had gotten fifteen minutes down the road to deliver today's special; what a sweetheart.

This was my first "away game" diaper change, and I assessed my options. I could handle this inside the store and roll the dice on whether or not the men's room had a changing table. I could recline the front seat back to make an operating table *or* push it all the way forward and use the floorboard in the back. Even better, pop the hatch, pull out the stroller, and use the trunk.

It had been a while since I'd done any tailgating. This was the sad, evolved state of a once-cool time.

In high school, tailgating was a couple of guys huddled around the back of my '85 Ford Ranger at the Hosensack railroad tracks in the dead of summer, shotgunning a case of Natty Lights we stole from someone's open garage. We'd toss the empties into the fire, hit a couple sprays of Binaca, and head to the Coopersburg Diner for a drunken midnight breakfast with the rest of our senior class.

In college, things changed again. If it were a sporting event, instead of shotgunning a car-keyed pounder, we upgraded to bottles covered with monogrammed fraternity Koozies. We had the aluminum Weber, an American classic with the porcelain-enameled bowl and rustproof ash catcher. We feasted on value-pack steaks, Jersey sweet corn, and hobo veggie packs. You could almost guarantee the grill master (me) would be donning the communal novelty penis apron while cooking.

The concert tailgate was a different species altogether. In the mid to late nineties, I hit a few dozen Phish shows over two summers. My laid-back attitude preferred tepid Sierra Nevada Pale Ales, the Holy Grail of parking lot beers. They did a good job washing down the hash brownies. The compact Coleman two-burner was the weapon of choice because propane was cheaper than charcoal, plus I'd found it on sale. I roamed the grounds in my crusty corduroys, trading hemp necklaces and hugs for a grilled cheese or veggie burrito.

After college, I entered the young professional step on the tailgating evolutionary chart. It was all about microbrews and twenty-one-year-old single-malt whiskey. We graduated to the Viking Ultra-Premium TruSear infrared burner that was so sexy. It may well have torched the pants off of the women. We popped our polo collars and experimented on filets with homemade dry rubs, while sipping out of cherished yard glasses that came from Williams-Sonoma.

But now, as a dad, tailgating has taken a new form. My first experience wasn't at Veterans Stadium or the sunbaked fields of Loring Air Force Base but rather a parking lot of the Babies "R" Us. There were no hooter shooters, no tossing of the Frisbees or smell of hickory smoke. Instead there was a blown-out-shit diaper, a stained onesie, and a panicked new father.

I set up shop on the fly toward the rear of the parking lot, popped the hatch, and used the back as a triage staging area to conduct business. I was admittedly a bit anxious, trying not to show any negative emotion as I went through the process. It probably wouldn't have been that bad, but I got flustered seeing people driving by, slowing down to take in the spectacle.

Parents, smiling because they've "been there, done that." As well as the car full of joker teenagers who'd skipped school and were out for a "high ride," all passing by from the confines of their air-conditioned cabins.

The wind picked up, and I had a mini-tornado of dirty baby wipes swirling around my head like the plastic bag in *American Beauty*. I had dust in my eyes, and if that wasn't enough, I fumbled her sucker, which hit the asphalt. If you've never tried to chase down a sucker that's hit the pavement, then you wouldn't understand why I was jumping around like I was manning up on zone D, eventually having to get down on my stomach with my tattered pride in the middle of the parking lot to reach under the exhaust of the car to retrieve it.

I cleaned off the sucker, closed the tabs on the diaper, wiped my eyes free of dust, and continued with my goal of returning this disgusting Diaper Genie. I felt weird, but I had to get over it. This was the new me. Changing crap bombs and hiking into a Babies "R" Us with a KO'd dirty diaper holder under my arm in the middle of the morning on a Wednesday.

Every part of me assumed that I'd be walking right back out through those doors, Genie in hand, denied of the return.

As I approached customer service, I set my item on the floor, and when asked, I presented it by sliding it across the floor behind the counter with my foot. In all reality, it was destroyed. I had accidentally punched a hole through it. If you looked closely, you could probably find remnants of turd smear. I explained that it had somehow broken and I needed to exchange it.

It didn't even faze this dude.

He handed me the store credit. "No problem. Do you need someone to show you where they are?" he said.

"Nope. I'm good." And with that, we were off to wander.

Wait. A. Second. Half of this store is a Toys "R" Us. Game on.

BLOCKING OUT THE NEGATIVE

We entered the store and I wiggled through the aisles with Ava in the Björn, navigating to the girls' toy section. I occupied her with a Malibu Barbie and took stock of everything around me. My initial scan turned up something huge.

LEGOs.

My generation had fought tooth and nail collecting G.I. Joe action figures, Transformers, and these beautiful interlocking plastic blocks. This consumed my childhood until I graduated into baseball cards. A youthful exuberance invaded my body, and I felt like Tom Hanks dancing with that kid on the giant piano in FAO Schwarz.

I'd spent endless hours constructing LEGOs as a kid. If I got bored of what the instructions told me to build, I took it all apart and came up with my own creations. I had started to acquire the City collection when it first came out in the

1980s and was blown away to see that it was still alive and kicking.

Mental degradation body-slammed my common sense in the middle of the toy store. Suddenly, I wasn't worried about the economy or the fact that I didn't have another job lined up. I had found my happy place.

We went to the front of the store and grabbed (again, out of antiseptic wipes) a shopping cart. I frantically loaded up pieces of the City collection into the cart as if I were a contestant on a game show.

That first trip, we spent around three hundred dollars to get myself started. I bought the farm (literally) and the updated fire department. I threw in a sports car and a few vehicles from the police department for good measure. The cashier suggested that my daughter was too young to put these together. I offered a sinister laugh and made her well aware these were for me.

After unexpectedly losing my job, coupled with the fact that I couldn't find anything new while adjusting to becoming a full-time caregiver, I had suffered from a bout of depression. I'd started on Lexapro, thinking it would get me through this rough patch.

But maybe these little blocks could be a replacement for the antidepressant. For the first time in weeks, I had a skip in my step and was looking forward to something. Sure, this could be slightly abnormal for a now thirty-four-year-old man, but I was so fired up to get home, the cops would have to set up a spike-strip checkpoint to stop me from getting to my living room to build.

I laid Ava down for her afternoon nap and made an attempt to tear open my new treasures.

If you've bought LEGOs before, you know that within the boxes come little plastic bags that contain all of the parts. If there are two things that don't mix, they're "opening plastic bags" and "babies napping." I was forced to go back into our bedroom, burrow deep into the closet to open all of these bags in an effort not to wake Ava up.

I hijacked the wooden bed-and-breakfast tray that sat on the buffet collecting dust and declared it a "building tray."

I sat down with some lemonade and began to piece everything together, thinking about this small community that I would soon lord over. It would, however, need a home. I couldn't just display these around the house like some bullshit tchotchkes.

I required a central area to flaunt my hours of "follow the directions" architecture. I conducted a survey of the house, walked the interior perimeter, and looked for a suitable piece of property to break ground on.

The dining room table. It was perfect. It was as if the heavens had split the clouds and cast a light on the table. I banished the fake orchid centerpiece from our wedding to the corner of the room and rolled up the place mats like congratulatory cigars. I yanked out the table leaves, extending my land grant to almost four feet wide by twelve feet long. From a lording perspective, this was a perfect grid to start with.

I put together my first round of purchases, sitting in front of the table like Russell Crowe in *A Beautiful Mind*, starting to envision potential streets and traffic patterns. My head was flooded with matrix code. I saw stoplights, fire hydrants, and a park for me to walk my LEGO dogs on lunch break.

I went online immediately and ordered a slew of individual green rectangles to create the illusion of vast rolling hills with elevation gain. I needed some smooth pieces to mimic sidewalks and blue pieces to create the pond within the park.

The police car was the last assembly of the day. I took it for a spin down Main Street and was in total control. There was a new sheriff in town.

Ava woke up from her nap, and I pulled together a home-made dinner just as Jen walked in the door from work. She might have been caught up in the excitement of seeing me clean-shaven, wearing a collared shirt and oven mitts, be-cause she didn't immediately notice my newly constructed community.

I started serving our food, and she questioned why we were eating off of the ottoman instead of the table. I noncha-lantly pointed toward the dining room with a mouthful of food and said, "I have a little project going on in there. No big deal." With her curiosity piqued, she peeked her head around the corner. I wasn't entirely certain that she was go-ing to fully embrace my new hobby. In fact, I can't imagine many wives would. But she did.

She caught me off guard by laughing and commenting on how cool everything was.

Days and weeks passed, and I extended the aggressive buying spree, adding big-ticket items like the hard-to-find Green Grocer and Grand Emporium. The buildings had three and four levels, complete with revolving doors, balco-nies, and fruit stands. I added some fields on the east end, a wind turbine and park with benches for people to sit and watch the koi.

I guess because I'd felt like I didn't have any control in my life, I enjoyed having control over this one. I had created the perfect plastic microcosm. I kept the police and fire departments busy, staging car wrecks and house fires, taking some real-life frustrations out in an alternate reality. The only caveat was that I had to lower my volume as Ava slept, but I still managed to integrate some sound effects into my playtime.

Jen's initially supportive attitude quickly changed to concern as I ordered more and more accessories: trees, flowers, lampposts, and stoplights. I joined the LEGO club for the quarterly points, got a free T-shirt, and was inundated with paper catalogs and e-mails. It became awkward for her to explain to our friends that we couldn't have them over for dinner because I'd taken over the dining room area with toys mainly marketed for young children.

Her patience waned, and I had to do something drastic to keep her on board until I was content with the city's condition, which would probably be never. Maybe I had taken this a bit too far.

I should've made reservations at our favorite restaurant or picked up flowers while she was at work. Maybe I should've ordered something naughty from Frederick's of Hollywood or bought her a mani/pedi.

Instead of lighting some aromatic candles and fixing a warm bath to take her mind off of things, I instead decided to offer her a position on the city planning board. I hoped that she might take an interest in helping me better the aesthetics of the city. Once again, she obliged and gave me her input on my creation. Her first move? She might want to rezone the entire city off of our dining room table.

Since Ava was born and I had lost my job, I didn't go out as much and really saw my friends only on special occasions. They were working full-time and also trying to start families of their own. One day, over the summer with the LEGO city at full strength, I invited my longtime friend Mark over to watch the Phillies game on MLB Extra Innings. We've known each other since we were thirteen, and I knew he would shoot me straight on my latest endeavor.

Our conversation went something like this:

MARK: So what's been going on, man? How are you?

ME: I'm great, bro. Ava is doing well. Still looking for a job . . . no real solid leads right now. Let me show you something I've been working on before the game starts.

MARK: Sure; sounds good.

ME: So . . . here it is. What do you think?

MARK: HOLY. SHIT. How much did this cost you?

ME: About two grand?

MARK: HOLY. FUCKING. SHIT. What is wrong with you?

We briefly discussed whether or not I was on medication, but we got interrupted by a knock at the front door. I handed Ava to Mark for a minute while I went to the door. I explained that it was probably the UPS guy, delivering a new batch of plastic trees I had been waiting for. Mark looked dumbfounded, standing in my dining room, surrounded by an out-landish city of blocks.

We agreed that this was cool but also uncool at the same time. He suggested that, yes, perhaps I had taken it too far and should maybe pump the brakes.

Jen was a good sport through all this, but she had decided to quit her job as city planner. She'd stopped offering me suggestions, and there was a bit of distance growing between us. I was so wrapped up in playing God over this pile of blocks that I ignored everything and everyone around me.

The romance had fizzled, and I was out of touch with reality. I should've picked up on the fact that this had gotten out of control. I was thirty-four and had spent an absurd amount of money to create something I was missing in my life.

I didn't expect to be here, doing what I was doing, and didn't necessarily have a choice in becoming a stay-at-home parent. I had never considered it as an option and wasn't confident I was wired well enough to handle it.

Finally I had control of something. Unfortunately, it was an inanimate object. I thought about all of this and also picked up on Mark's concern. Within a week, I quietly surrendered. I dismantled everything and tucked it away in clear plastic bins that I took to our storage unit.

I still go and visit the LEGOs, sometimes staring through the containers, waiting for the day we'll be reunited. Like the day I move our last kid into their college dorm.

THE INTERLOPER

Being a stay-at-home parent was starting to become lonely. Sure, everyone loves to focus on the obvious benefits. My friends would make me feel guilty and punctuate the idea that I got to build forts, eat Popsicles, and watch cartoons all day. It wouldn't be half bad if that were the truth.

Anytime I even came close to complaining about my situation, someone was always right there telling me that they would trade with me in a second or kill for my job. Really? You're looking to be thrown into a new job in which you're responsible for the life of another human being? You want to battle occasional depression and question your self-worth? You would actually kill someone to be in a position where you're changing diapers out of the trunk of your car and can't take a shit without an audience?

I'd be lying if I told you that there weren't a few days peppered in where we were lazy and we did overheat the DVD player and make pillow forts, but for the welfare of both Ava and myself, mentally and physically, I certainly couldn't live each day like that.

Finally it hit me. Like with any other job I'd had before, networking was the key to survival. It was a way to get to know my peers, trade information, and occasionally help one another out. But who were my peers? Day care administrators? Nannies? Other stay-at-home parents?

Networking while I was in the entertainment business came easy to me, and a lot of the time was done over a beer or a martini paid for by the corporate card. Not only was it easy to make friends, but I'd even met my wife on one of those corporate-funded drink dates. Our field was gender neutral. It didn't matter if you were a man or a woman, and generally speaking, so long as you had passion and aspired to excel within show business, everyone was there to welcome you into conversation and to the party with open arms.

But this was different. It wasn't realistic to take my kids to bars or comedy clubs to meet other parents. I couldn't spend our grocery money on a handle of Belvedere and break out a travel-sized martini shaker while pushing my kids on the swings. I mean, I could . . . but I certainly wouldn't last long before being incarcerated.

I was stepping into the stay-at-home parenting octagon with mostly women. Of course, there have always been a handful of stay-at-home dads over the years, but this had long been the ladies' territory. Maybe it was the carryover sixties mentality of where I was raised or media's societal expectations of years past, but there seemed to be a residual negative stigma attached to a man staying at home, taking care of the kids, doing the cooking and cleaning.

I'd soon learn that achieving a personal comfort level as a stay-at-home dad wasn't just about me having a few successful conversations with the neighborhood moms. In order to really make some headway, I'd have to reintegrate myself into society.

To be successful, I would have to sneak back through and pull a "reverse glass ceiling." For years, the women's movement struggled to break up the corporate boys' clubs and find inclusion in business fields they were very capable of succeeding in. In theory, I was doing the same thing and, very similarly, it wasn't going to be easy.

My first few efforts to get out there and mingle were hugely unsuccessful. I was no stranger to the hairy eyeball that were two or three moms on the playground, looking at the quiet, grown man standing on the periphery of the playground with his hands in his pockets.

I was constantly made to feel like I was doing something wrong and shouldn't be there. I quickly learned to establish with them that I was a legitimate father and one of these kids was mine before people's paranoia turned against me.

After a few visits, they probably realized I wasn't just down there on an occasional babysitting gig or my day off. Once the moms at my local playground saw me more often, they started coming closer, sniffing me out like a wounded bird being reintroduced to my habitat. It wasn't until I stepped in one day to butterfly-bandage the split forehead of one of their sons that they finally realized, not only might I have something to offer, but more important, I was one of them.

Until I got to know them a little better, I felt like I had to politely accept the unsolicited advice that came in waves. Occasionally, something might've been helpful, but in general it was stuff I already had experience with or was just being lazy about. The manner in which they delivered advice was all too often condescending. "Maybe she needs a nap" or "You do know that your daughter's shirt is on inside out, right?"

Because of those societal expectations of the past, men have been expected to provide financially, remain emotionally unavailable, and keep our cool without ever showing any self-doubt. It's created a negative workspace for us, with women watching everything we do microscopically. The pressure is insane.

I eventually bonded with some of these women and looked forward to seeing them day in and day out. Funny how, in the beginning, when we didn't interact, we hit the playground in our shorts or yoga pants, T-shirt or hoodie. Now that any apprehension was lifted and trust was established, I found myself wearing jeans, their hair was suddenly straightened, and I'm pretty sure I saw some mascara enter the scene. There was a little bit of middle school flirting as we playfully fought one another for mayorship of the playground on Foursquare. We picnicked together on our blankets and every once in a while took the kids to lunch down the street.

That's when I first noticed another hurdle involved with entering an occupation where men were generally overlooked. There weren't changing tables in the men's restrooms. I'd never really thought about it until I really needed one. While I'd like to think this was an honest oversight instead of a strategic money-saving decision, it said everything that didn't need to be said.

As the moms in my neighborhood and I began to realize, we weren't so different after all.

MY TWO DADS

With construction halted and the LEGO city in storage, I didn't really have a reason to stick around the house so much. I had to get back to my original mandate of getting out of the house once a day.

My brother lived only a few miles away, and I thought that an uncle outing was in order, so I arranged to pick him up.

The truth was, the days got lonely, especially since all of my friends were at work. While I was okay hanging around with their wives, it was nice to have my brother close by.

He was a twenty-six-year-old bachelor bartender and not completely familiar with my new lifestyle, so I figured it'd be nice to have a visit and give him a taste of the action.

I thought it might be fun to take Ava to the Aquarium of the Pacific in Long Beach to walk around, check out life underwater and, most important, get outside and add some pigment to our pasty skin.

Travis and I are eight years apart. I had graduated from high school and already gone away to college by the time he was ten. I didn't really get to know him through his teenage years, and once he moved west to Los Angeles in his twenties, it took a little while for us to get to know each other again.

I thought it might be good for Trav and me to have some hang time, but it was also an opportunity for him to bond with his niece. And since he was the in-house bar therapist at a cougar hideout in Venice, I could use a forty-five-minute car ride to hear about his customers' collective sexual conquests to make me feel like I was still in the game.

After I picked him up, we stopped at a local breakfast joint to grab a few sandwiches before hitting the road. It didn't take long to realize he was a regular there, as the Korean owners started shouting at him as soon as we walked in, addressing him as "Mr. Butters." Who would've guessed that my brother was the Norm Peterson of the egg sandwich place?

The first time he'd gone in for a sandwich, he'd ordered the #1, a bacon, egg, and cheese on a bagel. Unbeknownst to him, it comes with mayo, which he hates. Evidently, they're not used to special requests, and each time after, when Trav asked to substitute butter for mayo, he was assigned the "Meesta Buttas" nickname. It's hardly an award-winning story, but somehow it made its way into this book.

The owners didn't make much conversation, and it was awkward as we waited for our eggs to be cooked, listening to them replace popular song lyrics with the words "Meesta Buttas," as they sang the two words over and over again.

We ate our sandwiches as I merged onto the 405 south, which was an asshole factory by nine thirty a.m. We missed the calculated lawlessness of the first rush hour and were into the second shift, senior citizens out refilling prescriptions, landscaping crews, and java-fueled parents reaching behind the seat of their minivans to swat at their kids while bouncing in and out of the carpool lane.

Our conversation in the front seat started to sound like an old Dice Clay routine with Ava in the backseat sponging it up, so I faded some Radiohead lullabies to the back, in hopes it would drown out the various improprieties.

As we pulled up to the parking lot, I confirmed to myself (and my brother) that we had made an epic decision by visiting on a weekday. I went on and on about it as we drove around the empty parking structure, choosing one of the many elevator-adjacent spots.

It was one of those magical moments where we were in the museum after hours by ourselves. Kids in a candy store. We noodled around like we were on vacation, taking our time to pose for pictures in front of the aquatic-themed elevator entrance. We emerged on the bottom floor and approached the aquarium when it hit us like a pie in the face.

Was it National Field Trip Day?

Fourteen giant yellow school buses, parked in tandem around the pickup/drop-off loop. In between those buses and the entrance were hundreds of screaming elementary schoolers in loosely formed groups with a half dozen overwhelmed chaperones. It was chaos personified. Their clipboards and whistles were like pissing on a five-alarm fire, absolutely useless.

Trav and I discussed our options. We had come this far and our instincts told us that none of the kids had gone inside yet. If we pulled a Usain Bolt to the ticket window, we'd have a head start on them through the exhibits and still salvage a halfway peaceful outing.

Running in a loaded Björn is like one Siamese twin running a race while the other one just hangs around watching. Nevertheless, I lowered my head and awkwardly gunned it toward will call.

We picked up our tickets and scrambled for the lobby, where we realized that our instincts were garbage. It reminded me of being stuck in the hallway in between classes. Half of the kids had already gone in, and what we'd seen outside was the second wave of hyperactive tweens.

CHAPERONE: It's so great what you guys are doing. I'm so happy for you!

ME TO MY BROTHER AS WE WALKED AWAY: What the hell was that lady talking about?

MY BROTHER AND I TO EACH OTHER: Oooooooh.

It had taken only about fifteen minutes for us to be mistaken for a pair of gay dads by one of the chaperones.

We decided to put a few feet in between us and stop holding hands (kidding), because we were clearly sending mixed signals.

These chaperones were in the weeds. I haven't seen someone get worked over this bad since Kimbo Slice. It was supervised anarchy. As we dodged an ongoing game of tag that was dragging through the Southern Pacific exhibit, I was witness to at least one successful pantsing of a young scholar, who promptly yanked his sweats up and went into a full-blown mixed martial arts rage on his buddy. I snapped one picture of a fish as my brother and I shared a simultaneous look of concern with a dash of panic, not for this young man's self-esteem, but rather that we'd paid twenty-two dollars each for tickets to a preadolescent mosh pit.

We whizzed through the Sea Otter Habitat and Shark Lagoon with kids bouncing off of us like meteorites. As we turned our final corner, a crazy middle-aged ginger with superthin scarecrow hair came at me like she was gonna take my wallet.

Without hesitation, she started touching Ava's face, which threw me into panic mode. I knew she wasn't going to like it, but I powered up a core trunk rotation and blasted right through her. Travis was my lead blocker as we pushed through the crowd for the first down marker that was the exit.

I was bummed that we had to skip Lorikeet Forest, but I probably would've commanded those birds like falcons, to go and peck out the eyes of all those little brats. Once outside, we considered asking for a refund, but the immediate solace of the car was the winning voice on our shoulders. As we weaved our way out of the parking structure . . .

ME (looking at Travis): You all right?

TRAVIS: Yeah, I think so.

ME: Sorry, man. That was brutal.

TRAVIS: Can you pull over real quick? I
                          think I need a cigarette.

I've become used to this madness in the last year as a
SAHD. As I sat in the car, watching him pace back and forth
outside, trying to piece it together, I felt bad for Travis, who
may have been left permanently scarred and now may never
have kids of his own.

TAKE OUR KID, PLEASE?

It had probably been about six months since Jen and I'd had any time to ourselves whatsoever. I suppose we could've hired a babysitter here and there, but after watching all the hidden nanny-cam stings on *20/20* and *Dateline*, we were thoroughly freaked out.

Our good friends Mark and Melissa were tying the knot in Santa Barbara, which was about an hour and a half north of L.A. It was a quick trip and didn't require the hassle of getting on an airplane or staying overnight.

The reception was at the Four Seasons just off the beach, and we both thought it would be a perfect opportunity for us to have some alone time. We already decided that we weren't going to spend the night, but would rather find someone other than a babysitter who might stay with Ava for a few hours. It just so happened that our friend Shelene lived only five minutes off the freeway in Calabasas and offered to have Ava stay with her family for the evening.

I guess I had become something of an overprotective helicopter parent. It wasn't just because I was with Ava the most, but rather because I was a stay-at-home dad. I feel like there's more pressure on us because we are fewer in numbers. We're under the microscope more often, monitored to make sure we're doing it right.

After we brought Ava into the house, I continued to move her in. I brought her Pack 'n Play and two bags full of emergency items, even though she'd be there for only five or six hours, most of which time she would be sleeping.

Shelene had two kids of her own, but that didn't stop me from going through my list of Ava particulars. I had a very detailed checklist in my head that I began to rattle off. Jen looked a little surprised at my thoroughness, interrupted me, and reassured me that Shelene didn't need any of this information—she wasn't a high school babysitter and we weren't leaving for a week.

I always thought that Jen would be the one who would be worried out of her mind, unable to have a good time, when we left Ava alone with someone else, but it was me. I was insisting that Shelene text us pictures, updates, and if there were *any* problems, please call me.

As we left, I probably should've been catcalling out the window while doing a burnout, crushing beer cans on my head and coercing my wife for road head since I rarely got any time without the child. But I'm a class act, so I didn't.

It felt weird to get back into the car without the baby. I had experienced a similar feeling before, during the day while Jen was at work. I would constantly double-check to make sure that I hadn't left our kid in the parking lot, strapped into a shopping cart, or on top of the car after lunch. This was clearly a preferred reality.

There was a unique silence as we pulled out of the neighborhood and onto the highway. I still had residual qualms about leaving her, since it was our first time, but Jen convinced me that Shelene was more than capable and I should let it go and enjoy the moment.

We enjoyed the quiet for the next hour as we made our way to the hotel. As we pulled up, we relished the view of the ocean. We joined our friends on an outside veranda for cocktail hour and immediately dove into grown-up conversations.

I went out of my way to ensure the conversations didn't involve kids. I tried to make every conversation about the other person for once. Forget about me. I want to know what *you* are doing, what *you* are up to these days. So? Tell me everything!

The cocktail waitress was making her way around with hors d'oeuvres and beverages, and I flagged her down with every new tray she debuted. I truly wanted to tackle her through the doorway and pour martinis all over my face while shoving a dozen crab puffs into my mouth like I was on bath salts, but I remained calm. This was only a short break of adult time we had, and before too long, we'd have to be responsible and get back on the road and pick Ava up to go home.

As we sat through dinner, I keep bugging my wife to see if she had heard any updates from our friend. Why no updates? What was going on? My mind started to take a dark turn. What if they're in the middle of putting her on Craigslist or we end up getting a picture of her tied to a crib mattress with ransom demands?

We skipped dancing, but not dessert. We savored the cheesecake, said good-bye to the bride and groom, and had the valet bring the car around. I'll admit, I was a bit jealous of the rest of our kidless friends who were staying at the hotel overnight.

We ended the evening and drove back to Calabasas to get Ava. Turns out that all of my twisted thoughts and concerns were completely unfounded. Big surprise. She had played with the other kids, watched a movie, had a bottle, and fallen asleep.

What an asshole this kid was. She didn't even miss us? Such bullshit.

It was amazing what a few hours away had done for us. We had cocktails and adult conversations. We managed to have an entire meal without interruptions (aside from the best man toast). There wasn't a boob hauled onto the dinner table or a scramble to find a place other than the dance floor to change a baby. The only preoccupation was with each other. In fact, I'm pretty sure we even held hands for a minute.

All in all, it felt like we might be able to do this again sometime soon.

CHAPTER 6

A New Frontier

A PIERCING SCREAM

From time to time I can't help but remind my wife that, intentionally or not, she'd withheld certain genetic information about herself before we got married. She never disclosed her bum hip until the honeymoon was over and had also done a pretty fair job of hiding her second alien toe, which is longer than the others. She claims it's a sign of intelligence, but I'll argue that it somehow enhances her stubbornness. She also misled me on other vital information, which was that she'd been bald until she was two or three years old. I'm pretty sure that's something you mention along the way when you're having a kid with someone.

I did my best to coordinate outfits that worked in vibrant colors with flowers and butterflies. Despite my efforts, it took only a few errands around town to encounter a handful of oblivious A-holes asking me how old my son was. That, coupled with a few Facebook posts of my off days, with my daughter dressed like a vagrant, was enough for my wife to intervene and come up with an aggressive style-recovery plan.

When Ava was born, someone gave us a chronologically ordered box of Stella McCartney onesies that had the days of the week embroidered on the front.

These were brilliant, because I was stuck in the time continuum that is being a stay-at-home parent, with the days and nights bleeding together to form one long day that lasted several months, and currently, years. They helped me remember when the DirecTV bill was due and also made it super easy for the fashion illiterate to pick Ava's outfit for the day. Seven onesies will take you only so far before they're overridden with milk stains and purple yogurt.

Jen decided that we needed to cut down on the onesies and get some cute dresses and accessories to help Ava's cause. These would be our crutch until we talked about getting her ears pierced. Cute dresses were fine, but Jen *really* took the accessorizing and ran with it.

The elaborate Jamie Rae flower hats, sunglasses, and matching footwear combos started to look like Richard Simmons and Elton John had exploded onto our kid.

Trips outside of the house instantly became more complicated as I emerged from my car with a living, breathing Crayola color palette stuffed into a Björn and attached to my chest.

The downside of her looking like a Depression-era flapper from the movie *Chicago* is that it tends to create this weird power of human magnetism.

My kid became bait on a hook, and it seemed as if we

were out charter fishing for grandmothers and pregnant women all the time. Even without really trying, I caught a ton and hit our limit every time we left the dock.

It's almost as if there was some sort of unspoken obligation or a sign on my back inviting everyone in to invade our personal space and sneak attack us with "coochee-coos" and cheek pinches. We defended ourselves with the ever-reliant, often-recurring Elderly Heisman, brushing off nosy seniors since 2009.

Even with Operation Roy G Biv, we still had the occasional moron congratulating me on a boy to keep my last name alive.

Jen had called around to research several places that do ear piercing for children in an effort to finally put an end to these annoying instances of mistaken identity.

I had never really considered the whole piercing ritual/rite of passage. I grew up in a family of four men and my outnumbered mom. There weren't a lot of "girl issues" that came up. I went through the late-eighties and early-nineties fads of pegging our pants and piercing our ears, but I used an ice cube and a safety pin and felt like I was old enough to make the decision for myself.

What was the temperature out there for girls getting their ears pierced? I had noticed several babies with their ears pierced before and didn't really think anything of it. Earrings generally look nice, and I rarely considered the process in which they got there.

I had assumed that we would wait until Ava was old enough to make that choice herself, but I guess not.

My wife has two sisters, and they'd all had their ears pierced when they were only a few months old. As far as I know, the reasoning was that at that age it was too early to remember having it done, and the girls didn't have the dexterity to pull out the earrings. By the time any of them knew what was in their ears, they'd just assume the earrings were part of their bodies and play with them less, not be trying to rip them out. Sometimes people just follow the tradition of what they know.

My mother-in-law happened to be out for a visit at the time, and I think my wife planned it that way so we could all go and do this together. I can see how that would be nice for a mother and daughter to relive that experience together with the next generation.

My mother-in-law and wife insisted that I tag along. I admired the nostalgic attitude and of course I wanted to go along. I appreciated the invitation.

A lot of times your pediatrician will perform the piercing, but ours did not. In searching around, Jen found a few novelty earring stores that offered a piercing with the purchase of Ava's first set.

We started our day by going to Claire's at the mall in South Bay. They performed the piercings, but didn't have a great selection of earrings—plus, it was my wife's nightmare.

I don't think Jen wanted to let some punk teen pierce Ava; plus, everything they had was too long for Ava's thin, little lobes.

At this point, I had been driving around a good part of the day with no real ultimate destination with my screaming daughter, wife, and mother-in-law. I suggested that maybe we postpone our journey for the day and try again the following weekend. Not happening. Jen had this all planned out in her head. She had her game face on, and we wouldn't rest until it was done.

With the morning already burned, I decided to pull over and get everyone to hop on their phones and call some different locations to check on earring inventory. We finally nailed down the spot.

Unfortunately, it was in Glendale and we were in the South Bay. Even though it was only twenty miles or so, it might as well have been a trip to the moon. Four freeways, surface street shortcuts, a few gridlocks, and two hours later we pulled into the parking garage. Just one more reason that I'll never buy an "I love L.A." T-shirt.

We unloaded the car and made our way upstairs to the kiosk. There were several cute earrings in their collection, and we let Ava pick out her favorite. I think she was under the impression that she was buying a toy, not something that was going to be injected into an appendage on her head. We liked the silver hearts, but Easter was coming up and they also had bunnies, so we went with those.

As we moved through an explanation of the process and how it would go down, we came to the part where someone needed to hold Ava still. Both my wife and mother-in-law looked over at me.

I finally realized why I was here. I should've seen it coming.

Because I was with her day in and day out, Ava was comfortable with me and I didn't really feel like I had a choice on this one. I sat down on the stool with her in my lap as the technician cleaned and prepared the gun.

The emphasis was to keep her as still as possible because this was a one-time deal. They had already played the "this is a pretty marker; let's color a dot on your ear" game and now it was time to pay the piper.

There really wasn't a delicate manner in which to subdue

a baby, and I think Ava started to realize that something not good was probably happening here, so we needed to make it quick.

So there I sat, in the middle of the Glendale Galleria with my daughter in a headlock while she screamed her face off, as the window-shopping church crowd gawked and gasped. I know she wasn't screaming in pain because it started as soon as the strange tech sat down in front of her.

It took only four seconds and was done. I was pushed to the side as the collective hugging and sobbing mess that was my wife, mother-in-law, and daughter floundered around inside of the kiosk.

I'd had no idea what I was getting myself into and felt that I had earned a five-minute walk by myself.

The upside was that Ava looked extremely cute with her new earrings and was perfectly happy again after a few minutes. I wasn't certain how I felt about my role in all of this and started to wonder if I was beginning to see a pattern.

First the vaccines, now the piercing. Was it just a dad's role to handle these painful moments? Was I overreacting? Ava wasn't old enough for Jen and me to start pulling the good-cop, bad-cop routine, right?

I've got to wear a lot of hats being a stay-at-home dad. Maybe I couldn't be the good guy all the time. If I worked in an office all day and saw my daughter only at night and on the weekends, I'd certainly feel like doing anything to keep her happy, but our situation is somewhat nontraditional. Right now and moving forward, I'm a major influence on her. I'm with her ten to twelve hours a day. I can't be just one thing. I can't act just one way. I have to teach her what's right and wrong. And if she breaks rules, I'll unfortunately need to enforce appropriate punishments. I'll undoubtedly be one of her best friends, but occasionally, I'll have to also be her worst enemy.

I worked so hard at being the good guy every day that I finally started to realize the complicated emotional spectrum that is being a father.

PETER COTTONTAIL ON ACID

My mom chased the holiday traditions all year round. It wasn't just Christmas. At the beginning of every April, she would pull the Easter decorations down from the attic.

Easter Sunday at my house was treated much like Christmas day. My brothers and I would lie quietly in our beds in different rooms upstairs, waiting for my parents to give us the go-ahead to come down and discover what Peter Cottontail had left for us.

We spent the day before in an assembly line at the kitchen table boiling and decorating eggs, writing "dick" or "ass" on them with a wax crayon and handing them down the line to our mom to drop them in the various dyes. I guess her reaction to the defaced eggs was payback for making us sit for pictures, year in and year out, on a furry pervert's lap.

We would let the eggs cool and leave them behind to be

hidden. It was inevitable that we would find only twenty-three of the twenty-four eggs, leaving a single hard-boiled sulfur grenade to linger, undiscovered, somewhere in the house. Days later, as we sat around choking down egg salad sandwiches, we heard a loud "damn it" from the foyer as my dad put his toes through a rotten egg, stuffed into his house slipper, solving the mystery of the twenty-fourth egg.

After the egg hunt, before we escorted my mom to church, my brothers and I were sent upstairs to get gussied up for the annual Easter picture at the side of the house, where once again my dad's brickwork served as the backdrop.

My brothers got jerked around for years with suspenders, but I was able to get away with my go-to, every-season, all-occasion blue blazer. The three of us, unfortunately, were a casualty to the matching red clip-on ties, which haunted us for several years. We stood at attention as best we could, pleading for the picture to be taken, as we succumbed to direct sunlight and ragweed allergies.

Ava was a little young for a full-on egg hunt this year, but that didn't mean she couldn't enjoy her basket. In a lot of homes, these baskets were probably saturated with jelly beans, Peeps, and chocolate bunnies.

My Easter basket was apparently assembled by a hippie flower child, choosing to focus on clear skin and a cavity-free mouth, leaving me with cheese, carob chips, and dehydrated apple rings.

In retrospect, it was probably a smart move that preemptively avoided a post-church sugar-induced frenzy among three prepubescent boys.

Since this was Ava's first Easter and she could barely eat solids, aside from one obligatory box of Peeps, the sugary tradition would have to wait another year. As I sat there watching her, I realized that she couldn't care less about the fancy treasure trove of bunny socks, onesies, stuffed Hello Kittys, pink glitter Toms, and Care Bear DVDs tucked inside the basket. She was completely blown away by the piece of crinkly plastic that surrounded it, and I started to wonder if maybe the Easter Bunny could've gotten away with less.

After opening her basket, we drove to the mall to relive another anxiety-ridden moment of my childhood, the lap photo with the Easter Bunny himself.

In the late seventies, without giving me much of a choice, my parents subjected me to a strung-out, psychedelic *Alice in Wonderland* version of Peter Cottontail. The overpowering smell of Old Spice on his stained bow tie forced me to close my eyes, sit on his lap, and hope he wouldn't pull me down the rabbit hole with his soiled lint-balled pink mittens, exposing me to his after-hours party of rodents sacked out on dirty sofas surrounded by black lights.

I nearly pissed my pants the first time around, silently chanting the "there's no place like home" mantra in my head, forcing out a grin to my mom exuberantly waving from the sidelines.

Thirty years later, I found myself taking my daughter for her first prized photograph and, once again, I noticed that times had changed. Ava seemed to get a softer, less emotionally rattling bunny.

He sat on a handcrafted wooden bench with his floppy story-time ears and round-rimmed glasses, donning a suave midnight blue smoking jacket. There was an abundance of natural light, spring flowers, and the laughter of children emanating from the food court. The advancements in digital technology had us in and out like greased lightning, and it was far less traumatic than I remembered.

The excitement of Easter had come to an end and Ava passed out in the backseat, wearing her bunny ears. And I made it through the holiday without finding an egg in any of my footwear.

PONY UP

Over the next few weeks, Ava's eyes lit up every time we brought up bunnies, and she seemed to really have a new affection toward the rest of her stuffed animals.

As the weather warmed up, we started going back to the Venice Farmers Market. We milled around the vendors in a giant circle, watching people elbow and shove one another to get to the free samples of super-aged cheese and homemade pesto. It was quite an eclectic mix of farmers, yuppies, hipsters, and granolas, uniting to show off their recycled tote bags, eat corn on the cob, and trade patchouli hugs.

And then there was me. I was in my own category. The sweaty, exhausted, now slightly out-of-shape dad, running back and forth to the car, pumping quarters into a parking meter to avoid the seventy-five-dollar ticket.

I pushed the stroller through a packed marketplace, trying not to bruise the ankles of everyone in front of me while craning my neck off into the distance to ogle some freshly made crepes. Everyone was in their own world, including me, having a relaxing Sunday morning free of big decisions.

But that would quickly change as we made the mistake of turning down the aisle toward the front side of the market, where they hid the pony rides and the petting zoo. Once I realized where I was, it was too late. Ava had already seen the prize. There was no turning back.

My wife is a sucker for the photo op, and I knew immediately I wasn't getting out of this. Ava was pointing toward the ponies with her finger, making cooing noises, and it was impossible to turn away and let her down. There were four ponies walking in a circle with their trainers, attached to a metal carousel. So much for our calming day without major decisions. I was hesitant to put her on a pony because she was still so little.

Jen offered to walk alongside her, leaving me to battle it out on the sidelines in awkward small talk with a bevy of hipster dads in skinny jeans and vests.

I watched the trainer buckle Ava into her harness and started to have some second thoughts. What if this thing got spooked, reared back like Tonto's horse, Scout, and took off with my kid down Main Street? Who has the liability insurance around here? Does State Farm have my back on this one?

I guess since everyone else seemed to be jumping off the bridge, we would, too. Ava was on sensory overload, watching the pony in front of her push out steamers onto the wood chips, pointing and yelling "poo" while doing 360s around a crowd of parents taking pictures.

The handlers weren't charging anyone for the rides and, instead, were just asking for donations. Let me hop up on my soapbox for a minute. Asking for donations is the biggest scam in the book. Just give me a price! Don't make me do the "guilt times generosity" equation.

Preying on that guilt and making me look like a cheap asshole in front of everyone gets them more than they would charge anyway. Maybe that scam is a pretty good business model . . . I handed over ten bucks.

As I looked at Ava smiling, having a great time, I couldn't help but think about how I might have royally screwed myself down the road. The only likely outcome from this experience was for her to eventually ask Dad for a pony for Christmas or her birthday.

Between the vaccinations and piercing pagoda, I was already sweating how much of an asshole she'd think I was. I couldn't afford the damn pony she's gonna want.

I didn't have pony money lying around; plus, I'm pretty sure our homeowners association would have some beef about a horse grazing off the flower beds. And what happens when she outgrows it and wants to upgrade to a Budweiser Clydesdale? All of these hypotheticals and this new image of their furry hooves put beer on my mind.

BJURINATION

The farmers market is just off of the Main Street drag in Venice and Santa Monica. It's a mile of shops and restaurants lining both sides of the street. Jen suggested that since it wasn't naptime yet, maybe we should put Ava in the Björn and walk up and down a bit and do some window shopping. Window shopping is *never* window shopping, but so long as no one was selling horses, I agreed.

I was still getting accustomed to the baby carrier, and it seemed like every time I went to put it on, my wife had been wearing it last, meaning every strap needed to be adjusted.

We looked like a real pair. My wife was holding Ava while I did the human tornado in the parking lot. I spun around and around trying to find the armholes. Almost like an old cartoon where the dog chases its tail, my arms were chasing my body.

From the other side of the lot, I probably looked like a seizure victim, with my hands bound by a twisted strap, while I continued to yank back and forth trying to free myself. I grew sweaty and flustered, but determined to Houdini my way out of this baby straitjacket without the help of my lovely assistant-wife.

Ten minutes, a near mental breakdown, and five pounds of lost water weight later, I was set up and ready to holster our little equestrian.

The older Ava got, the less tolerant she was of hanging in midair from my chest. Between her kicking or grabbing anything within her jurisdiction and people stopping us to engage in cutesy baby talk, we were lucky to get anything done at all.

As we finished touring one side of the street, we realized that Ava was asleep. We thought it might be a good opportunity to pop into the Irish pub for a burger and that beer I was thinking about. If we were lucky, she'd sleep right through it and we'd just continue on our little journey. If we weren't, well, I guess that's why they invented takeout containers.

We strolled into the bar, and it was as if a record had scratched in the middle of the big dance. I pulled up two stools at the bar and had a seat.

The regular seated next to me turned and said, "Well, you see something new every damn day."

I found it hard to believe that I was the first guy to stop into the pub with a kid on his chest, but maybe I was setting the trend. We ordered some hefeweizens and burgers, and Jen said that since Ava was asleep and I had everything under control (wink, wink), she was going to "pop next door" to look at something.

A few minutes had gone by and I realized that I really had to go to the bathroom. My options were few. Either give my sleeping infant over to "Whiskey Sour Paul" or continue into the bathroom and negotiate taking a piss with her hanging from the Björn. I chose the latter.

I made my way back into the bathroom and decided which I would use, the feed trough urinal or the actual bathroom stall. Considering my clearance issues and the idea that I wanted to keep Ava sleeping, I chose the trough.

Ava's feet split the "work area" to the left and right perfectly, and even though I couldn't see anything, I'd be fine. It was a little bit like Malkovich putting together that gun under the table to shoot the president in *In the Line of Fire*, except I wasn't killing anyone, just taking a leak.

As I'm midstream, the door opens. I turn to see what's up, and another patron had walked in on my operation with a dumbfounded look on his face.

I gave him the standard "What's going on, man?" He laughed and countered with a "Holy shit, dude. Wow. Haven't seen that one before," and moved on to the stall. What I didn't realize was that as I'd turned to acknowledge this guy, the bottom of my T-shirt had fallen down and I had finished my piss on the inside of my shirt.

The expletives gushed softly from my mouth, and I quietly managed to rinse the bottom of my shirt in the sink, all the while with Ava hanging in the balance. I then tried to use the blower to dry whatever part of the shirt I could, not thinking about the fact that it made the noise of a fucking fighter jet taking off six inches from your face.

Ava awoke to find herself suspended over a wind tunnel in the men's room of an Irish pub. Let's just say that she wasn't too happy. The hysterics were initiated, so I made my way back to the bar.

By this time, Jen was back and seated on the stool waiting for us. As I emerged from the back room, my midsection completely soaking wet, with a screaming kid, her face went blank.

JEN: What happened? I was gone only ten minutes.

ME: Nothing. Just forget about it.

BARTENDER: And here are your burgers. Sorry they took a minute.

JEN: Wait. What happened while I was gone?

ME TO BARTENDER: Can we actually get those to go?

JEN: Adrian?

And that's how we handled it. So many things happen throughout the course of a day with a baby that sometimes no explanation is the best explanation.

DAD IS ALIVE

I eventually told my wife what I had attempted that day in the pub. She laughed hysterically at the story and suggested that maybe I start a blog and talk openly about some of these funny moments.

The truth was, despite how much I got out of the house every day or switched up my routine, I was a little down about my situation.

Never in a million years had I thought I'd be a full-time stay-at-home parent. I had always seen myself as the one bringing home the bacon and acting more like a deputy to the sheriff when it came to parenting.

Even though this recession had put nearly twice as many men as women out of work, I wasn't necessarily seeing it on the street. It was still very much a "wives' club" at the playgrounds, parks, and recreation facilities.

Maybe there were other guys out there going through the same thing. Maybe it was a good idea to find a forum to vent my frustrations.

My pride, self-esteem, and self-confidence had all taken a hit. This wasn't me. I'd never had a problem with those things in the past. I was always proud of the work I'd done and been able to measure my successes.

I didn't acknowledge the contributions that I was making to our family. I couldn't see the forest from the trees. I was fighting not to slip into a deeper depression. I wasn't getting a weekly paycheck and, at a certain point, I felt like I'd lost my sense of authority and input on what we did or how we spent our money.

I went through the motions of paying bills and running the household, but I felt like a stranger. When my wife came home and we got Ava to bed, I'd go for the wine. I was drinking to escape.

I really ached inside. After spending more than a decade being completely submerged in the world of comedy, I needed some laughter back in my life. It was the one thing that could really turn my ship around, and I think my wife knew it.

I took her advice about starting a blog, and one night while I made dinner, we brainstormed about potential names. A lot of them had already been taken, but unbelievably, Dad or Alive wasn't. I couldn't believe it. It sounded so obvious that I jumped at it.

Over the next few weeks, I had completely changed my attitude toward my situation. This project had me excited and feeling invigorated. I asked my friend Jeff to help me with the design and implementation of the Web destination. I started to explore an entire subculture of not just stay-at-home moms, but dads as well. Despite me not seeing them represented as heavily out on the playing field, they *were* out there.

I treated the endeavor like a job. It was exactly what I needed. It would help me find the humor in my everyday struggle of being a fish out of water, as well as add more structure to my day.

I had taken so many pictures over Ava's first eight or nine months and documented that time so well that I thought it was only fitting to start from the beginning.

As time progressed, I gained more followers, shared content, and interacted with other parents online, and it started to actually feel like what I was doing had substance. It might sound silly, but reading comments and seeing retweets was giving me a boost in the self-esteem and confidence departments.

With the help of the Facebook and Twitter parenting communities, as well as the support from my wife and my mom, I began to realize that what I was doing *was* important. In fact, I had an opportunity to do one of the most important jobs there was, raising a child.

Perhaps it was because Ava was so young and I hadn't really seen much feedback or evolution in her personality or development, but those defining traits and physical changes were slowly happening.

My confidence and esteem were boosted, and I made a decision to be the best I could at my job. To be the best parent I could be. The payoff would exceed the value of any check I could take to the bank.

In writing about my experiences and sharing my joy and frustration, I could see that I wasn't the only one in my position.

The grim reality was that because of the shitty state of the economy, I might not go back to work in the field I loved anytime soon, but maybe I had found a way to continue peddling laughs.

The Internet loves when you tell the truth, and I was committed to putting it all out there. I felt like there was a limited male perspective on being a parent and I could help. Raising children isn't only a woman's job, and the emphasis on dads doing their part is even more relevant today.

I kept up with the blog during Ava's naps and late at night. I had found a creative outlet. I completely reinvented myself and felt like it was all turning around.

I love sharing my experiences with Ava and putting it all out there, but sometimes a tiny part of me wishes I'd done it anonymously.

Jen loves to introduce me to people in public, mention that I should tell them about my blog, and walk away, leaving me to make parenting sound exciting to someone I don't even know.

I wonder, when my daughter is old enough to understand privacy, media, and the Internet, if she'll be mad at me for putting her birth and childhood out there for public consumption. *Or* . . . if she'll adore and cherish the fact that I took the time to document our adventures together. Adventures that she'll likely be too young to remember.

Regardless of the outcome, Dad or Alive was born and I finally had somewhere to put my parenting angst.

CHAPTER 7
Wild and Unruly

CRYING OVER SPILLED MILK

Around the time that Ava was nine or ten months old, things really started to happen quickly. Up until this point, my job was relatively simple. I'd move her around from the Bumbo seat to the swing to the Pack 'n Play, trying to stimulate her imagination and hold her attention. It was a relatively low-maintenance routine, which suited me just fine.

I knew that Jen was toying with the idea of weaning Ava off of breast milk. I just wasn't sure when. Jen was comfortable with the amount of time that she had breastfed Ava, and though I don't know what it's truly like, I'm sure that having to lock yourself in the office conference room or a bathroom stall at work to pump the milk out of your canteens could grow old after a while.

In the meantime, while Jen was at work and the frozen breast milk was dwindling, I had slowly introduced Ava to organic formula and milk and took a stab at purees and spoon-feeding, too. I'm a "routine guy," and it kind of sucked a little bit, to get one down and then have to change it as soon as it got comfortable. But as I would learn, I shouldn't get comfortable with anything, because raising a child is nonstop evolution.

During the day, I worked on the formula and puree transition every few hours, but at night after Jen got home, it was breastfeeding time. It was great that Jen and the baby could take the time to bond, and on a more selfish note, it was an opportunity for me to have twenty minutes to myself.

They were also mini vacations, and I used the time for all sorts of things. I'd check the mail, walk the dog, make a phone call, or check the score of the ball game.

One of the upsides of her weaning was that the boobs would soon return home from war and be available for occasional recreational use. I'd have to arrange a lesson on etiquette, though, and speak with Ava about the condition in which she returns items she borrows, but nevertheless, this was a win for the good guys.

Around Ava's tenth month, from down the hall one night, I overheard Jen talking to Ava about how this would probably be the last nursing they would have together, and a few minutes later, my break was interrupted as she asked me to make a bottle.

It was my last twenty-minute furlough with no responsibility.

Certainly it was a mark in the win column, as we rapidly depleted the stockpile of frozen breast milk travel pillows in the freezer. We now had room for our old friends—ice cream and beer mugs.

With breastfeeding over, the breast pump would soon be tossed into the storage unit, saving us valuable kilowatts and certainly freeing Jen up from having to lock her office at lunch or hands-free pump while sitting in freeway gridlock.

More responsibility had fallen on me in the process though. Not only was I the primary caretaker, but now I was also a novice chemist, adjusting and perfecting mixing ratios of water and powdered formula on a daily basis. I ditched the bottle warmer because, along with giving myself several third-degree steam burns, it simply took too long. When this kid was ready to eat, she was *ready to eat*. Instead, I ordered a five-gallon water dispenser that had the hot-water option. Instant gratification.

With less boob and more bottle, I also became a laundry expert. The molecular composition of the formula, while having milk, soy, and a bunch of "phates" and "trates" that provided vital nutrients, also could've been used by the Native Americans to permanently dye or stain garments.

I was now responsible for spraying down the collars and fronts of every onesie and outfit, but figured this out only after I hadn't treated the first batch, locking in those yellow stains and ruining them all.

I couldn't understand why Ava was so unhappy with some of her bottles. After some Googling, I learned that nipple flow seemed to be the cause. . . . It was time to upgrade to fast flow. I felt some déjà vu as I Googled nipples to learn more about the issue. The only difference this time around was that I didn't feel compelled to erase my browser history.

I continued my hand at spoon-feeding her purees, but Ava glossed right over them. I jumped to solids, cooking diced veggies, along with noodles. It was a constant game of guess and check. Half of what I tried ended up on the floor, and the dog was clocking overtime hours cleaning everything up.

Our carpet was taking a serious beating, and we were well on our way to losing a security deposit. Jen suggested that I purchase a splat mat. I had priced them and made the executive decision to forgo spending fifty bucks for a piece of plastic that's whole purpose was to be destroyed.

I headed down to Home Depot with my helper in tow, and for two bucks got us a plastic painters' drop cloth. It lacked some style, but this wasn't HGTV.

I tried to avoid turning Ava into a carbivore, but sometimes it was just an easier option. In the off-meal times, I sometimes gave her puffs, teething biscuits, and crackers, as they were clean alternatives to blueberries and raspberries.

What I didn't know was that once she mushed these together in her mouth and formed a paste, they could and would be smeared onto her toys and into any open crevices.

If I missed a smear during cleanup and it dried, it may as well be Quikrete, fastening the heads of dolls together like Siamese twins and forcing me to break out the hammer and chisel during naptime.

THE GREAT ESCAPE

Ava's food regimen wasn't the only thing keeping me on my toes. She had gone from scooting to crawling to full-on walking within a few short weeks around her ten-month birthday.

On a normal Friday, Jen was already at work and I had laid a blanket pallet down on the floor for Ava to lie on. I surrounded her with toys and rolled-up blankets as bumpers so she couldn't squirm past them. I turned on Nick Jr. and went about my business, making the bed and collecting laundry to be done.

It took me a few trips back and forth to the washer before I realized that the pallet was empty. What the hell? Where was she? Had someone come in here and swiped her as I whistled while I worked?

I panicked, as she was no longer in the living room. I sprang into action, sweeping my eyes from corner to corner.

I flew into the bathroom and found that she had rolled or crawled her way up against the base of the toilet, a good twenty feet from where she had started.

I knew I had to do something to avoid having this happen again. The last thing I needed was for her to end up on the balcony or down the hall. We ran to the store, and I picked up a baby jail. It was a collapsible octagon that looked fit to hold small kids or animals. Hopefully, this would contain her.

The following week, I resumed my daily chores with Ava duking it out against her toys in the circle of death. As I came out of the bedroom, I realized that she had summited the top of the jail and was precariously teetering on the top. It looked as if she were poised on the top ropes, about to bring an atomic leg drop upon her Lalaloopsy doll. Any sudden movements and she might take this entire plastic octagon down with her.

Two weeks, and the jail could no longer hold her. She was a mini Lou Ferrigno, her little legs bulging and ready to tear through her onesie. Her ten-month-old legs wanted to walk, and there was little I could do to stop them.

In a matter of days, she was standing and hopping from sofa to shelf and room to room, using anything she could hang on to to make her moves. It was happening too fast. A month ago she could barely move. I used to be able to set down coffee or anything I wanted without having to worry about it (or her) walking away.

I was bragging about Ava's achievements on Facebook, and people commented on the fact that we'd need to fully baby-proof the apartment.

What did that mean?

The vodka was already out of reach in the freezer. Did I need to lock up the *Kama Sutra* handbook too?

As I read the comments online, Jen called from work and told me that she'd need to leave on business for a week. And she was flying out tomorrow.

Was she out of her mind? How could she leave me alone with this critter? She was now fully mobile, and nothing in our apartment was nailed down. This would be a true test of what we were both made of. I kept a journal about our time together during that week.

It went something like this:

SUNDAY: Ava's afternoon nap was a fake out. It lasted about fifteen minutes, then turned into tossing, turning, and waving at me through the video monitor. After bringing her to the living room, I noticed that she's seriously disinterested in watching the Pro Bowl with me. She wants *Backyardigans*. We fight over whose show goes on the tiny thumbnail smart window.

MONDAY: While unloading dishes in the kitchen, I notice a suspicious silence. The red flags go up, as this is the main indicator for a potential situation. Trouble confirmed after I find Ava dragging red and blue crayons, All-American style, along the walls throughout three different rooms. The wet rag treatment resulted in massive smearing. Added "buy paint" to my to-do list.

TUESDAY: Naptime is once again a bust. Is this kid doing meth? Why won't she lie down? Nightfall offers a bath-time surprise when a bundle of turds are jettisoned from her butt out into the water. Just before bed, I thought it would be a great idea to spill thousands of Israeli couscous across the countertop and onto the kitchen floor. Within seconds, Ava was enjoying mouthfuls of starchy, uncooked pasta beads.

WEDNESDAY: Ava takes a day off from the nap-boycotting movement but still doesn't let me off the hook. She instructs the dog to vomit on my foot while I'm wiping her down from lunch. Washed my foot off in the tub and added "carpet stain remover" to the list.

THURSDAY: Evidently the new trend is banging your head into the walls when you get upset. Considering giving it a try myself. Violent tantrum includes whipping her head back into mine, which results in a giant black eye for Dad.

AN ASSAULT ON THE KING

Jen was back in town from her trip east. She appeared well rested. Good for her.

I, on the other hand, was a scruffy and disheveled mess. The queen had left the castle, leaving us vulnerable to attack. I was doing everything I possibly could to fortify and defend it, as we were under siege.

I had done the necessary research on baby proofing, but it took me a few days to pick everything up. In the interim, we remained on high alert as the attack continued.

It started with my BlackBerry in the toilet. Then it was the infatuation with pumping water from the dispenser. Although it helped me warm those bottles quickly, maybe getting that thing wasn't the best idea. I'd remove Ava; she'd act uninterested for a moment until I was distracted and then go right back for it. I had to fashion a *MacGyver* rubber band and paper clip situation to stop the madness.

She discovered the on/off switches on the power strips and how to unplug the DVR and computer. She had uncovered some of my vintage *Playboys* from under the bed.

Mommy and Daddy's personal items within the nightstand were open season. I discovered a strip of Trojan condoms and a set of cuff links in one of her Hello Kitty purses.

The cleaners under the sink were heavily guarded (an obvious weakness), but she figured out how to use the remote to change the language of my favorite shows to Portuguese.

She was now tall enough and strong enough to hang on my shorts, pulling them to the ground while I did dishes.

It was a full-on assault.

I bought baby gates for every room and floor. I picked up doorknob protectors and cabinet locks and even found a lock for the toilet seat. I got wind-up knobs for the window blinds to keep the strings up high.

Once one problem was solved, another was born.

Now I was the one who couldn't get into anything. I had locked myself out of everything. My hands were constantly cut and blistered from trying to get into the pantry and open children's Tylenol that I could barely get the toilet open fast enough on most occasions.

I had become a prisoner in my own home.

MOUTH LIKE A TRUCKER

Ava was adapting and learning quicker than I could keep up. She possessed an alien intelligence that stayed one step ahead of me.

It didn't stop at excelling physically. She was sucking the knowledge from everything around her. Between cable programming, me reading her stories, and her eavesdropping on everything we said, it was only a matter of time before my wife and I would be defeated for good.

She was identifying objects and associating them with their names. She was curious about everything.

It was a regular Tuesday, and Jen had left for work. Normally, I'd take a shower while she was still at home and get everything set up so that my sole focus for the rest of the day would be Ava instead of cleaning or organizing.

Since I'd missed my chance to shower solo today, I had to

bring Ava into the bathroom with me. I'll never forget this day. The night before had been the last time that I'd ever use the toilet again without an audience.

From here on out, there was no peace.

She was handing me toys, asking me questions, messing stuff up that was out of my reach so I would have to hop off the john and ducky-waddle over to move it out of her reach. Then I'd have to get back to the toilet fast enough so her bait 'n' switch technique didn't work and she didn't get the opportunity to put her arm in the water. What would normally take me seven minutes to do took around thirty.

I started the shower and undressed to hop in. Our child has seen me naked from time to time but had never been perceptive enough to communicate any concerns.

As I let the rushing water clog my ears and drown out the babbling, I managed to see her banging on the shower door, staring and pointing at my nether regions.

I kept a poker face and tried to avoid any type of reaction on my part, because quite honestly, I wasn't sure how to handle the situation. Finally I gave in.

"Are you looking at Dada's pee-pee?" I asked.

We had reached the point where I needed to exercise some modesty. I worked out a whole system of hiding behind hanging towels simply to avoid the attention.

I managed to cover myself and avoid any further staring at waist level, but things were going to have to change.

I finally got dressed and we prepared to take a trip to our local REI. They were having a seasonal sale, and I needed a few propane tanks for my camping stove. This was less of a priority and more of an excuse for me to get out of the house. We walked around for a bit, and I had found the tanks that I needed.

I stepped up to the cash register and placed my items on the counter. A cute girl in her twenties began chatting me up while Ava was dangling in the Björn. She was right in the middle of commenting on how well behaved and cute she had been when all of a sudden . . .

Ava belted out what sounded something like "Fuck me! Fuck me!"

The quantity and repetition picked up substantially, and I went from shrugging and laughing it off to a sheer panic. It had piqued the interest of everyone nearby as they stopped to look while the cashier began to blush. Why in the hell was she pulling this *Rain Man* shit on me now? This was so messed up.

She continued repeating the words as I tried to figure out what the problem was. It was like she was malfunctioning.

In my head, I was flipping through every parenting idea I had. Was her leg pinched in the Björn? Dirty diaper? Hungry? Tourette's?

Who had she heard this from and where? How was I going to write this down in her baby book as "first words"? I had already made up my mind that it had to be her mom.

She began pointing down toward the waistline of the hot cashier. Could she be a prodigal child and pieced together the birds-and-bees equation by seeing Mom and Dad naked a few times in the shower? Is that why she was yelling "fuck me" and pointing at the employee's vagina? As I looked down, I realized that she wasn't saying "fuck me," but rather trying to say "froggy."

I exhaled and went out of my way to issue apologies and make sure everyone around knew that she wasn't being raised on the set of a porn shoot. She was smart and able to identify the stuffed frog key chain, rather than picking up foul language she'd overheard from her mom.

I got her to the car, buckled her in, and sat in the front seat, with my head on the steering wheel, taking a minute to recount what had just happened. From the backseat, Ava said, "Dada, froggy."

I turned to realize that in all of the embarrassing confusion, she had reached out and stolen one of the frogs from the counter.

"Froggy," I said out loud. "Fuck me," I said to myself.

CHAPTER 8

Discomfort Zone

ALL DOLLED UP

Everything was moving so quickly now, I was already fast-forwarding to moments down the road when she would be wearing makeup and skirts, dating boys, going to dances, and wanting to stay out late with my car, and it was giving me gray hair.

Ava was ten or eleven months old, had her ears pierced, and was wearing dresses. Jen was brushing her teeth at night, combing her hair, and she had high-heel shoes to dress up in. She walked around the house, imitating my wife with her lipsticks and makeup and filling her purses with a thousand things, exactly like her mommy.

Her personality had blossomed so much in the past two months. She was able to point and pick things out that she liked, and I was giving her choices on what outfits she might want to wear each day.

I became a little apprehensive about letting her grow up too fast and just wanted her to slow down and be a child. I really didn't want her to be one of those kids on *Toddlers & Tiaras* and was very paranoid after reading articles about how companies are trying to sexualize kids—girls in particular—before they even become teenagers.

Ava was starting to take a real interest in dolls, and her Memaw and Pop told us they had bought her an American Girl doll for her upcoming birthday. Jen suggested that we drive over to The Grove, an outdoor mall, and visit one of their locations to familiarize ourselves with their accessories.

ME: I'm sorry. Did you just say "familiarize ourselves with their accessories"?

JEN: She's a big girl now. She's into her dolls.

ME: Babe, you know we're back in baseball season and the game comes on at one.

JEN: Don't be an ass. Your daughter is more important than the Phillies.

ME: Wait. What? Why do you have to say it like that? No one was pitting them against each other! Whatever. Let's go.

Women can be really sneaky sometimes.

I had no idea what American Girl was or why it was such a big deal. I had just assumed it was a store that sold a few dolls. That Saturday we got ready to go, and Ava came out of her room dressed in a plaid Burberry dress with matching beret. WTF was happening? Were we going shopping in the south of France or what?

Part of me wondered if we'd be doing stuff like this if we'd had a boy instead of a girl. Would we be dressing him up like a construction worker to go and get surf and turf at Sizzler?

Evidently, this was a big event for Team Girl. We were going to let her pick out some accessories for her doll. I was trying to contain my excitement, as difficult as it was.

We parked and walked in the direction of the store. I kept my eyes peeled for a tiny little boutique doll shop, trying not to miss it. And in that instant, like an oasis rising out of the desert, there it was. Grandiose and obnoxiously large, American Girl.

We entered the lobby, and there were teams of mother and daughters, some dressed the same, all holding one or several dolls in their hands.

There were kiosks where we could make a hair appointment for the doll at fifty bucks a pop. There was an armed security guard greeting patrons, and there were prototype dolls behind glass cases like they were the Hope Diamond.

"Let's go upstairs and check out some stuff," my wife said.

Seriously? There was another floor of this insanity? Ava was obviously very happy, and I was excited for her until I started to peek at the price tags. I found myself in a potentially hypocritical position because of my previous LEGO addiction (the cost of my city was now north of two thousand) and didn't have much wiggle room to put the kibosh on any purchases.

I was trying to be patient and let the girls shop, but we had been in there for over an hour and were in danger of missing a lunch with some friends and their daughter. (The game was DVR'd remotely from my iPhone.)

I tried to tell Ava that we needed to go, but she wasn't having it. I offered to buy her the accessories that she'd picked out, but that wasn't enough. We had brought her to a doll store and she wanted a doll.

That pretty little piece of sunshine that left the house in her fancy beret was now a squirming, rowdy heap on the floor of the store. Screaming and kicking her legs, she was a little less American Girl and a little more *American Psycho*.

I implored my wife to take over the negotiations on how we would convince Ava to compose herself and walk out of this store. It took a litany of bribes, including snacks to be determined later, and she finally stopped crying.

We walked to the car and I looked at my wife and said, "I guess big girls *do* cry, don't they?"

PAPA'S GOT A BRAND-NEW BAG

Fresh off the outing at American Girl, we went to meet some friends for brunch.

Brunch is a fake meal between breakfast and lunch, most likely made up years ago by parents who wanted to take advantage of that peaceful time of the morning before lunch and naptime.

Our friends had a beautiful daughter a few months younger than Ava, and it was nice to get together, compare notes, and reassure one another that no one had gone completely bat-shit nuts yet.

Since everyone at the table was currently employed except for me, I felt like I really needed to shine. I drove through the parking structure, staring straight ahead, thinking about how I was going to bring my A-game.

I would talk about how I'm trying to teach Ava how to

swim, learn her ABCs and 123s and say "please" and "thank
you." Perfectly good examples of what she should be learning, but not too far-fetched that I'll come off as annoying,
trying to one-up them.

I acted invincible—unaffected and unfazed—when it
came to talking about teething tantrums and growing pains.
As far as they were concerned, it all bounced off of my emotional armor and made the whole table feel like I totally had
my ducks in a row. Either that, or I was a complete liar.

Forty minutes after we ordered, the food finally arrived,
and herein was our first problem. Forty minutes in a restaurant with two babies and no food is like being ball-gagged and
waterboarded at Guantánamo. We tried to maintain a conversation while throwing small distractions to the lions. A honey
packet here, a spoon or creamer there, anything to keep them
sidetracked from the fact that we weren't eating yet.

After a few words with the manager, the food finally arrived. I thought we were in the clear until my wife's side of
hollandaise came out like an ice cube. Between the kids'
growing impatient and the doubled wait time, we'd expected
a flawless meal. And since it had taken them so long, it made
no sense that anything should be cold. Jen takes her food seriously and ignited on our waiter like a pack of Black Cats
stuffed in someone's mailbox on Independence Day. We all
traded small talk with our kids until the exchange was over.

The manager clearly had kids of her own and felt horrible
about the confusion. She came over and took care of the bill
for the table, and I figured that our day had been turned
around. We calmed down, ate our meals, and continued the
conversation.

I had a pretty good gig going until Jen decided that she
needed to dig through *my* diaper bag to find something for Ava.

I don't care who you are, the diaper bag sometimes gets neglected. For me, this bag was the sarlacc from *Return of the Jedi*. It rested over my shoulder, waiting to take off anyone's hand that went in.

It's a multitentacled beast whose immense, gaping mouth is lined with several rows of sharp teeth and swallows anything I drop in there. It's a twenty-four-hour garbage disposal for my parental/toddler amenities.

At home, *she* has two beautiful Coach and Kate Spade bags, green and pink. They're both *clean*, have matching changing pads, golden clasps for the shoulder hitch, and a stuffy uptown demeanor.

My bag was given to me as a gift by some friends. It was one that they didn't use and I was happy to have it. As you know from our battle at the grocery store, it's green camo and serves its purpose well. I didn't need a ton of bells and whistles.

Forget about the fact that I have to wear it over my shoulder like a purse, the camo gave this thing balls. It looked used . . . ridden hard and put away wet. It didn't necessarily receive the same TLC that Jen's bags did. There could be days or weeks that my bag isn't cleaned out or tended to. There are only so many hours in the day and I'm only one man.

This is the one thing I had not thought about. The State of the Union of this bag was about to come down on me . . . hard.

I anticipated a disaster. As she fished through it, I fidgeted around, trying to think of excuses for everything she was going to find. I pile stuff on top of other stuff with a borderline hoarding mentality. It was a geologist's dream. Sedimentary layers of toys, perishables, and dirty diapers.

This brunch had turned on me. As Jen burrowed through my museum of trash and showcased everything on the table, I cringed in embarrassment in front of our friends. I mean, how bad could it be? So long as she didn't pull any dead hookers or coke out of my bag, I was safe, right?

She excavated it like some sort of forensic analyst. First it was diapers that were two sizes too small, from three months ago. Then it was the "missing" airflow bottle filled with what was once milk but was now a tube of curdled cottage cheese. As she got toward the bottom, she pulled out something that resembled a gray golf ball and held it in the air for the patrons to observe.

I'm not even certain what type of fruit it may have been in its previous life, but it was beyond mold and shriveled into a state of rigor mortis.

My friends (and onlookers) got a hearty laugh as Jen asked me what it was. I was sweating, feeling like it was the Daily Double and I needed to answer for the win. It looked like a shrunken head that shamans used for spell casting. I sat dumbfounded, smelling and squishing it. What is a petrified tangerine from the end of March? *Correct!* Now I just need Alex Trebek to cut to commercial and save me.

My A-game of parenting suddenly looked more like a C minus, with missed attendance and poor class participation.

The good times rolled on as we pulled out hospital rattles from '09, a spare outfit from the three-to-six-month category, and the Chex Mix shrapnel and broken Cheerios that covered the bottom. Everyone had a hearty laugh at my expense, which really set my "I'm a great stay-at-home Dad" campaign back by several years in one fell swoop.

SWIMMING WITH SHARTS

The Fourth of July had come and gone and we had laid low this year. Normally we would have cocktails, hop on our beach cruiser bikes, and head down to the Marina to lie directly underneath the barge that was pumping out the fireworks, to smell the gunpowder and experience the full explosions, with shrapnel snowing on our foreheads.

It's a little difficult to do that with a baby. But that didn't mean that we couldn't enjoy other activities now that summer was officially here.

Jen suggested that we introduce Ava to the swimming pool. I paused to digest that information and shot her a look as if someone had removed her brain from her head while she was sleeping.

Could you even do that? This kid is less than a year old. Wouldn't the chlorine in the water slough the skin off her bones like hydrochloric acid? Then what? Child services would be at our house in, like, ten minutes.

I could already see it. An aerial shot from the Channel 9 chopper at the top of the six o'clock news, with tanned poolgoers surrounding Ava, who now looked like Two-Face from *Batman*, with one of her eye sockets melted off and exposed. As they lead my sulking body away in handcuffs, Ava shoots me a look (with the good eye) that tells me when she's in her twenties and I'm finally out of prison, she'll be back to seek retribution.

Jen reeled me in to explain that it's never too early to introduce a baby to the pool and reminded me that Ava had floated in water for nine months. I tried to argue with the logic, but science always wins.

As far as the pool was concerned, my focus was on safety, whereas my wife's focus had shifted to Ava's attire. As a dude, I've swum in cutoff jeans (commence laughter), boxers, and have even gone commando when the situation deemed it necessary. I've swum in ponds, rivers, lakes, and oceans. It was never a huge production. Take off your shirt and dive in. There were no accessories or an entourage of gear.

Now I found myself bogged down with sunhats, water slippers, and pink duck towels. Half of the time my wife has Ava dressed like Liberace in one of his performance outfits, about to take the stage.

As we got ready to go down to the pool, I had serious concerns about reliving the extraordinary cinematic moment from *Caddyshack* when that kid released his bowels into the water, everyone yelling, "Doody!" and maintenance coming down to drain and disinfect an Olympic-sized swimming pool. I wanted to avoid any sharting incidents, and luckily my wife was already one step ahead of me. She had purchased waterproof swim diapers that would contain any such leakage, keeping our dignity intact and saving us from a potential PR nightmare.

We got Ava into the pool and swam around for a while, until I moved her into what was essentially a high chair for the water. There were a few things that she could chew on and the mesh netting kept her afloat while I amused her with my amateur backstroke and freestyle swimming moves that used to impress the ladies in junior high.

She got bored after about ten minutes, and Jen hopped into the pool to show me a trick she had been doing with her in the tub at home. I was curious what it might be and swam backward a few feet to get the full experience.

She held Ava, blew air in her face, and then dipped her underwater. I felt the laser beams on our necks coming from everyone's eyes around the pool. I could almost see swimmers diving for their cell phones to dial 911 and hear the rotors of the breaking news chopper creeping up over the hill, into our neighborhood.

Once again I looked at Jen like she had bumped her head. I sank halfway into the water and whispered to her that our neighbors probably thought she was trying to drown the poor child. She reluctantly told me I was paranoid, and as we plucked Ava from the water, we did a 360-degree pirouette for good measure, pretend-laughing and acting out a faux Norman Rockwell moment to calm the masses.

Ava didn't seem to mind getting dunked, and before too long, we were doing it together as a game. It doesn't change the fact that it had initially frightened the shit out of me, but for now, I know I'm better off just kicking back and relishing the fact that my daughter is still wearing a one-piece.

FIRST TIME FOR EVERYTHING

One thing we were excited about that summer was a wedding in Monterey in Northern California. It would be our first real road trip. We would drive eight hours north with Ava and the dog. The wedding was on Pebble Beach, and since we were up there, we'd stop off at the aquarium and let Ava visit the fish.

We loaded up the car, and I was curious to see how this drive would go. Ava was too young to really enjoy a DVD or use the iPad, so she basically had to sit still and stare into the back of my seat for a few hours.

It just so happened that our friends who were getting married had arranged for us to stay in a dorm room at the University of California, Monterey. The groom was an employee there, and we jumped at the chance to have a free place to stay. Plus, we had a friend in the area who was able to watch the dog during our stay, so it all made sense.

As we arrived on campus to unload the Pack 'n Play and take our air mattress upstairs, I felt a little nostalgic. This was the first time in almost fifteen years that I'd been on a college campus, and quite honestly, it was like the past and present were butting heads.

All of the classic dorm sights and smells were there: hints of burnt ramen and the unexplainable stains on the hallway carpeting. The communal area with the office-style furniture and bulky twelve-inch TV set. As I looked out the window into the woods, I saw a pair of running shorts in the weeds, some empty Boone's bottles, and a bag of something hanging from a branch. Typical.

I pumped up the air mattress and considered how this might play out. An air matty is tricky on your own. Adding my wife and now potentially Ava to the equation could get tricky.

The wedding was supposed to start in an hour, and it was a twenty-minute drive. We really needed to get showered and dressed. It felt like I was getting geared up to go out on campus for a kegger crawl, except for the fact that we were married and dragging a kid around with us.

We pulled ourselves together and hopped in the car to take the five-mile ride down to the beach. We parked on a hill at the top of the street and thought we would need to walk just a hundred yards on the sand down to the water. Ava was asleep, so I kept her in the Snap N Go car seat.

We walked toward the beach and hung a right, making our way up the sand to the ceremony. Every time we rounded a bluff or got over another sand dune, I realized that we were past the point of no return, yet the destination continued to seem farther and farther away.

I was ankle-deep in sand, with my pants rolled up, trudging on with my linen shirt and thirty-pound kid in a car seat.

I was a sweaty, drenched mess by the time we arrived to join the group of people getting married. The groom wore a kilt, and I could hear golfers playing above our heads on the golf course.

The ceremony was beautiful, and afterward, everyone headed back toward campus, where the reception was being held in the dining hall.

Jen and I stayed behind for a few minutes to take some pictures of us in our white and khaki outfits down by the water. She was shooting a video of Ava and me with our feet in the water, and her commentary included the fact that she was so excited that this was Ava's first time in the ocean.

The problem was that it wasn't. Several weeks earlier, I had taken Ava down to the beach at home to play in the water, and I had taken several self-portraits of us. I felt guilty about letting Jen go on and on about it, especially on a video that would most likely be sent to everyone we know.

I gently broke the news to her and immediately felt her disappointment. For so long, I had been focused on my own pity party, never really considering the fact that my wife had made sacrifices as well. She didn't have a choice as to whether or not she continued working full-time. She had to, or we would go under. In having no choice, she was forfeiting a large opportunity to be part of those new, everyday experiences.

The problem was, where was I supposed to draw the line on what we did together and what we did separately?

I mean, Ava's brand-new to this world. Anything that she does could potentially be her first time doing it. I just didn't know which experiences were more important than others.

We hiked back to the car. I had Ava in one arm and the car seat in the other, seaweed stuck in between my toes, and my linen shirt looked like a crumpled piece of paper.

Ava slept through the dinner and the subsequent reception, and we headed back to the dorm to get a good night's sleep. Being in an unfamiliar place, the baby refused to fall asleep in her crib, so we were forced to keep her between us. The fear of making noise by moving on the stupid mattress and thinking I might roll over and take out our whole family all made for a great night's sleep. I slept on my back like a pencil and tried not to move in my dreams.

The next day, I felt like I needed to make up for bursting Jen's balloon about the first-time beach visit and suggested we stop off at a few places on the way back to L.A.

We met our friend to pick up the dog, went to the Monterey Bay Aquarium, and had lunch. Because the first trip to the aquarium with my brother a few weeks back was such a disaster, lasted twenty minutes, and Ava never saw anything, we felt like we could pretend it hadn't happened and start fresh. The entire time, it was, "Awww, it's Ava's first time seeing an otter," or "Awww, it's Ava's first time seeing a jellyfish," or "Awww, it's Ava's first time eating French fries at the aquarium cafeteria."

As much as it was my idea, this was starting to get old. How many goddamned things could she do for the first time and how long were we going to announce them as such? I do stuff for the first time every day, and I'm in my thirties; no one is following me around putting everything on Facebook.

We stopped off in Castroville, the self-proclaimed artichoke capital of the world. Guess what. It was her first time here! We needed to get pictures of Ava with the steamed, canned, and fresh artichokes. We also needed a picture of her with the giant novelty artichoke out in front of the store.

We loaded our artichoke haul into the car and made our way south to Gilroy. Gilroy is a town you can smell from five miles away. That's because it's the self-proclaimed garlic capital of the world. Ava's first time there!

Now we're at a roadside stand sticking Ava in a giant bin of garlic cloves and have a garlic necklace around her head like she's preparing to fend off a team of vampires.

The firsties thing was getting really old at this point, and I wasn't sure how much more I could take. So what if I took her to the beach and she got her toes wet in the ocean? Was I going to have to hear about it for the rest of my life? I kept my thoughts to myself like a good husband, and we saddled up to continue the remainder of the trip, hopefully uninterrupted.

It was the middle of the afternoon and the temperatures had climbed into the upper nineties. The Interstate 5 south was pretty boring. It included a lot of rolling hillsides and open fields that could put you to sleep fast.

My wife had noticed a hand-painted sign that said FRESH BLUEBERRIES, PICK YOUR OWN on the side of the road, and I heard her mumble something about it from the passenger's seat.

After doing the aquarium, stopping for artichokes and garlic, and the scorching heat outside, this was the last damn thing I wanted to do. I changed the subject and hoped that she would forget about it.

As we continued driving, I saw the blueberry farm approaching on the left but hoped that if I didn't say anything or make any subtle movements, we would drive right by and she would never notice.

As we passed, my wife quickly perked up with "Wait. I thought we were stopping to pick blueberries. It would be Ava's first time!"

"But, honey, we already passed it, and there's a big patch of grass down the middle of the highway. I can't really turn around," I said.

"So you're not going to pull over," she stated (not asked).

Jesus. I couldn't stand the passive-aggressive stuff. I quickly pulled over, at which point, I put the car in reverse and used my mirrors to back up a few football fields. We finally made it to the entrance and pulled in.

I opened the door, only to be hit in the face with the hundred-degree heat. My pores opened up, and I was deluged with sweat.

Jen wanted to take our time and let this be a leisurely activity, even though I had secretly wanted to get home in time to watch a baseball game and we had several hours left in our trip.

I snaked my way into the Björn; we put on Ava's sunhat and picked up our blueberry pails at the station.

Ava and I moved up and down the aisles, picking blueberries (as quickly as I could) as Jen followed us with her camera, commenting on how it was Ava's first time picking blueberries. I was guessing it might also be her last. How painful was this?

I can see where picking apples might be fun. They're big, it doesn't take long, and we could probably make an apple pie later. Blueberries are tiny and I have big fingers. It's a labor-intensive process with little to no payoff.

Toward the end, or when Jen wasn't looking, I was just grabbing clusters of berries, ripe or not, and ripping them off the branch so we could fill our stupid pail and get the hell out of there.

I felt the beginning stages of heatstroke coming on and had also pandered to my wife's request sufficiently enough, so we headed back to pay for our berries.

We got back on the road, and I set the cruise control at eightyish to try and make up some time.

Jen asked me why I wasn't ever interested in suggesting a first time event that we could do together. I said that I just felt like she had it covered, but I would do my best to come up with something.

Perhaps it was time that I consider the fact that we spend so much time apart and we should plan more things together.

As we hit the Grapevine (a stretch of highway in Kern County) and came up over a hill, I moved into the left lane to pass another car. We had briefly crept over ninety miles per hour, but after I passed the vehicle, we dropped back down into cruise control. I exited the freeway to change to a different road and immediately realized we had a California Highway Patrol car in hot pursuit.

I couldn't fucking believe it.

While I was passing the car, Jen had noted that I was going too fast, especially with Ava in the car, which I was now painfully aware of.

The officer advised me that I was going ninety-three in a seventy-five. I asked him how he had even clocked me when he wasn't on the highway. I was politely calling bullshit. He pointed up in the air and said, "The plane got ya."

Sure, I was aware of the signs that said SPEED MONITORED BY AIRCRAFT, but I always thought those were a joke. I asked him to have the plane land because I wanted to see the proof.

He didn't necessarily appreciate that and continued to issue me a ticket.

He returned to his vehicle, and I sat behind the wheel with a stupid grin on my face.

Jen asked why I was so happy and why I felt the need to smile. I asked her to take a picture of Ava and me. Dumbfounded, she asked me why.

"Because it's Ava's first time being pulled over. By an airplane," I said smugly.

"Asshole," she mumbled as she took the picture.

HERE TODAY, GONE TONIGHT

The blueberry excursion had chewed up valuable time, and we were behind schedule to get home for the baseball game I wanted to see.

After driving for a few hours, being pulled over, hitting construction and traffic, Ava and the dog needed to stop, get out, use the bathroom, and stretch.

Lately, I'd gotten into a bad habit of putting things on top of the car while loading and unloading the vehicle. First I lost a pair of Ray-Bans at the hospital. Then it was three lattes in one week. I'd left bottles and even the breast milk cooler up there. All in all, I had already racked up a five-hundred-dollar bill in roof-related expenses.

On more than one occasion, other motorists had flagged me down. The first time, it caught me off guard, someone in the car next to me, yelling from behind a closed window, shaking their heads and pointing to the roof. After the second and third time, I knew exactly what was going on and issued a thumbs-up.

The sun was setting, and I pulled into a rest stop so I could walk the dog and Jen could change Ava. I thought I was doing her a favor by straightening up the backseat and unbuckling Ava so we could pull her out.

In doing so, I had placed Ava's only two satin "babies" on the roof, along with her favorite pink blanket. I walked Cooper and Jen handled diaper duty. We met back at the car a few minutes later and again I thought I was helping our situation.

I got the dog back in the car and took Ava from Jen, buckling her in and giving myself one last stretch before we got on the road to finish the last leg of our trip.

As I proceeded onto the freeway, Ava was in the back, slowly ramping up from a mumble to a scream, telling me that her baby was outside. I looked up through the panoramic moonroof and saw a flutter of pink as it launched into the air and into the night.

The mood in the car suddenly turned sour as Jen had realized what I'd done. Between the tractor trailers zipping by me, the yelling from the front and the back of the car, and trying to figure out how and where to pull over, I was ready to open the door and let myself out of the moving car.

I continued to the next exit and got back on the freeway headed to where we'd come from. Unfortunately, I had to get off again and on again to retrace my path. The speed limit was seventy, and as cars zipped by me, I crawled on the shoulder with my hazards on, looking for any sign of Ava's cherished fabrics.

Through the pitch-black of night, I noticed something

two lanes over that shimmered in the headlights. It wasn't another hoagie wrapper or grocery store circular. It was the pink blankie! I darted across two lanes and pulled into the grass in the middle of the highway.

I jumped out and ran to grab it. I got it back to the car and, upon investigation, realized it was a little worse for wear. There were several black marks on it, and when I handed it to Ava, she frowned a bit and gave me a funny look, complaining about how it was dirty. It would have to suffice.

I started to feel a little better about the whole situation, and even though it was my fault, I took pride in feeling like I'd saved the day by rescuing it. What we really needed, though, was one of those babies. Otherwise the rest of our ride home would be tough to handle.

I continued up the highway for about a half mile, trying to decipher the difference between used tissues and satin fabric. Jen alerted me to another shimmer of something off in the weeds. I pulled over and jumped out.

We had found one! This one didn't look like it had been run over, and despite its lack of cleanliness after being turned loose on the interstate, I handed it to Ava and smiled at Jen from outside the car as we shared a moment of relief.

JEN: What about her bottle?

ME: What bottle?

JEN: She had a full bottle at the rest stop.

I looked all over throughout the back of the car and couldn't locate it. Just as I was about to give up, I noticed it.

Still sitting on top of the car, wedged between the roof and the rack. It had survived up there for the duration of the rescue mission. I acted as if I had found it on the floor in the backseat as I handed it to my wife.

JEN: Thank God you didn't put that on the roof.

ME: Yeah. Thank God.

CHAPTER 9

It's Your Turn

A HAIRY SITUATION

That Monday after we got back from our weekend away, Jen returned to her grind and I was trying to figure out my week.

I had recently been pretty ballsy with my daily routine and felt like I could take Ava anywhere and she'd be fine.

I *really* needed a haircut, and I made an appointment, planning to take her with me. It wasn't like I was going to be in the chair for three hours to get a cut and color. A simple trim was all it was going to take.

It'd make me feel rejuvenated, refreshed, and hopefully, a little more relaxed.

We showed up for an eleven o'clock appointment, and Ava had already taken a short morning nap in the car, plus had a snack and milk. She had a fresh diaper on, so I felt like I had created the best-possible situation for her to be able to sit in her stroller for half an hour.

I got shampooed and conditioned (which I hadn't expected) and moved over to the chair for the cut. I parked Ava next to us and let Sylvia go to town. "Short on the sides and back and leave a little up front," I said. I had been getting the same cut for twenty years, every time, saying the same thing. I'm worried that those words are how I'll be remembered after I'm gone. I wouldn't be surprised if they etch them into my tombstone when I'm dead.

Ava did okay for about fifteen minutes, and then the wheels slowly started to come off. First it was fidgeting, then kicking and throwing things out of the stroller. It eventually graduated into screams, and I knew that this wasn't going to be the best environment for my stylist to proceed. It's never good when she says, "Don't worry. I'll hurry it up."

No! I didn't want her to hurry it up. Why couldn't Ava just sit still and let Daddy do *one thing* for himself? Did she sense that I was getting something to go my way?

I felt horrible as the salon helper came over, setting down her broom to pick up a shift of babysitting. Our chair became the epicenter of the action inside the salon. I was constantly twisting my head to the left to see what Ava was doing. These distractions couldn't be good for my hair. The receptionist was now involved, miming hand puppets, making it an official tag team.

Sylvia managed to finish up, and whatever relaxation I had gotten out of having my hair shampooed and conditioned was gone. I changed Ava's diaper on the sofa of the salon, thinking this was not the "pampering" I'd had in mind.

I started to ask myself questions in the car on the ride home. Jen was gone from eight in the morning until six or seven at night. Once home, she was thrilled to be with the baby, but I still had to finish dinner. By ten o'clock, when it was all said and done, I had blogs to write.

What time was I taking for myself? How was I supposed to retain my sanity and find a release every now and again?

By the time Jen got home every night, I found myself hiding in the bathroom for a few moments of silence. I'd walk the dog and take the long way around the neighborhood, relishing a few minutes to myself.

That weekend we went to a baby shower for some mutual friends. I started to gravitate toward my friends' wives, many of whom also stayed at home with the kids.

We congregated in the corner, and they were curious about how I was adjusting to being a stay-at-home parent. I tried to make it seem like I had it all under control and that it was a simple gig. They saw right through the bullshit and commented on how important it was to take a moment for myself, whether it was exercising, seeing a movie, or even going out to get a cup of coffee. Something. I had to do something to reset my perspective.

They had half jokingly mentioned that I should join them once a month for something they called "work drinks." It was an opportunity for them to leave the kids behind with their spouses and meet up to let loose.

As we drove home that night, I mulled it over in my head. At first I thought it was kind of silly for me go out for a night on the town with a bunch of my buddies' wives. But was it really that silly?

WORK DRINKS

I had decided that maybe this wasn't such a crazy idea after all.

I mentioned it to Jen, who found the idea funny and gave me her blessing. After we got home, I e-mailed the girls to see if their offer was serious and if it still stood.

Maybe this was some sort of secret society like the Freemasons. Instead of retired war vets getting blasted at the moose lodge, it would be a tightly wound network of MILFs knocking back chardonnay, giving one another breast exams in between having pillow fights.

I doubted my luck was that good.

We set the date, and my good friends (their husbands) put me on notice, faking me out with harassing voice mails indicating they were suspicious that I was going out with their wives.

They let me sweat it out for a few days, then let me down easy by telling me they found it absolutely hilarious that I was going to dinner with a bunch of moms. It was a little emasculating, but whatever, these girls would get me.

On the night of our rendezvous, I felt like a teenaged girl going to prom, walking around the house asking my wife which outfits (unfortunately, I did say outfits) looked better than others and testing out different colognes on my wrist.

She looked at me like I was an idiot and assured me I wasn't going to some secret orgy of the married wives and I "sure as shit wasn't getting laid." I was, however, taking pride in my appearance and wanted to look good, mainly because I spend most days in a milk-stained T-shirt and bathing suit. If nothing else, it was an excuse to dress in clean clothes.

I arrived at the wine bar they had chosen and noticed they had already saved a seat for me. I approached cautiously, not knowing whether to fist-bump or kiss cheeks. I was accustomed to beers at the bar with buddies, but this was spritzers at the wine bar with their wives. Casey and Nicci were there and had invited a single girlfriend, Gena, also a mutual friend, so it made a party of four.

They welcomed me to the table with a congratulatory cheer and explained that my initiation was to complain as much as I wanted. We loosened up with some drinks and it became a full-blown bitch session within the hour.

I worried about being lumped in with the working dads, hoping that I wouldn't feel like the target of their gripes. That wasn't the case. I was a stay-at-home parent just like them, going through a lot of the same struggles, only sometimes coming at it from a slightly different perspective.

We drank and reminisced about life before kids and I

tried not to let any stories of their husbands out of the safe, something that might jeopardize the reputation they've built at home over the years.

Instead I bit my tongue and gave them some gems from my single life, feeling like Samantha dishing to Carrie, Miranda, and Charlotte, huddled around the table, hanging on to all of the juicy details.

The conversation shifted to stitch-n-bitch mode. Unlike the crocheting WWII-era housewives before us, we dropped the needles for pint glasses but still managed to keep the bitching alive while we unloaded about being at home all day. These women all had boys whereas I had a girl.

I wondered if one was easier than the other. We shared similar experiences, but definitely not everything.

We all agreed to being open to drugging our kids with Benadryl to get them to sleep on an overnight flight. We knew which grocery stores took double coupons and had the enjoyment of scouring our child's room before bed, turning off the sounds of a hundred annoying, hidden toys. We knew where the good playgrounds and indoor gyms were and which bookstores had story hour and when.

Nicci versed me in the art of the thirty-minute power cleanup that's done just before your spouse arrives home. It gives the illusion of slaving over household chores all day.

We all bribed our kids to keep them content and from screaming in public. We'd turn the radio up or put the A/C on full blast so they would stay awake to get home for naptime.

Even though we weren't the breadwinners anymore, we agreed that we didn't feel less important to the marriage relationship. They reassured me that they didn't hold back with any spending on their end.

These women dealt with Pee-pee Teepees and avoiding a whizzing fire hose while changing diapers. They endured the awkwardness of walking around town with dried lactation spots on their T-shirts and pumping breast milk in the restroom of a crowded restaurant.

One time, in a pinch, Casey had to bring her son to a Brazilian waxing appointment. He started off at eye-level in the stroller, but as Mom was about to go spread eagle, the waxer suggested they turn him toward the wall for everyone's safety.

I began to think that maybe I had it easier. But the reality was that we each had our difficulties.

With no inherent fashion sense, I dealt with having to make Ava look cute in public and also took measures to shield her from seeing my balls in the shower. Aside from this particular night, cracking the wives' club was a tall task. The number of stay-at-home moms greatly outnumbers the dads and it's not easy to gain acceptance.

A moment of silence fell over the table as we all realized it was getting late and work drinks were almost done. The waitress had overheard our conversation throughout the night and thanked us for being her best table. She, too, was a stay-at-home parent (with a night job too) and felt our plight. She knocked the food off the bill and gave us a wink as she walked to the kitchen.

It wasn't the hedonism I had originally expected, but I did feel like one of the girls.

And I did get that moment to myself that was greatly needed.

MAN OVERBOARD

After hearing the girls tell me to take some time to myself, it just so happened that another opportunity came my way.

Jay, one of my groomsmen and a close friend, was getting married.

He had scheduled a weekend that was devoted solely to the end of his bachelorhood. At first I didn't think there was any way I was going to be able to do this. Jen worked seventy hours a week, and to dump Ava and the dog on her and take off to enjoy myself for the weekend might be a tall order.

I ran it by her and was a bit surprised when she didn't even seem fazed by the proposition.

My brother Travis was also invited, so we planned on making the trip together. The best man had arranged for a weekend in Santa Barbara. He had pulled out all the stops and rented an amazing house with all the amenities.

I was surprised that Travis would even consider going anywhere with me after the aquarium incident, but this was a much different beast.

It was really only one night away from home, but it was my first night away from home in almost a year. Jen didn't seem concerned initially, but as we got closer to the date, I think she started to realize that she was rolling solo for the weekend and I was going to get turbo-drunk somewhere with a bunch of dudes.

I did my best to downplay how much fun I was going to have and commended Ava and the dog on their recent behavior within earshot of Jen. I made it seem like her weekend would be a cakewalk.

I picked up my brother and we started our journey. It was the first time in a year that I'd been able to put the moonroof back, rock the stereo, and not look into the backseat and see baby accoutrements. It was Jay's weekend to be a bachelor, but I could certainly relate.

The unspoken theme of the weekend for me was "overboard." We went overboard on everything. Trav and I stopped at the grocery store before hitting the house and picked up some necessities: a few thirty-packs and handles of booze, a bag of hotdog buns, and some chips. This was all we needed to survive for the weekend.

When we pulled into the driveway, half of the guys were already there. The house was amazing. We threw our duffels down and didn't even take time to choose a room. The day drinking began and we mixed in circuit training of basketball, Frisbee, swimming, Jacuzzi, horseshoes, and playing catch in the yard.

I no longer had the stamina I did in college, and by

midafternoon I was a bit wobbly and worse for wear. I needed to pace myself if I was going to make it out on the town for drinks with everyone else.

By late afternoon, we all showered up and ate dinner at the house and got ready to board a shuttle bus that would take us onto the main drag. We had spent the entire day boozing, swimming, and playing games. As we sat on the bus, I started to feel guilty about having such a good time. It was around Ava's bedtime, and I thought about how Jen might be juggling everything at home. I left a message and we began our night on the town.

I began to think about the whole bar scene a little bit. Sure, it was awesome when I was single because that's where we went to meet up with girls. Now that I was married with a kid, aside from being out to celebrate with Jay, the bars didn't seem to make that much sense to me anymore. How much more could I drink? What was my goal here?

I've always had a built-in mechanism that tells me when I've had my fill and points me in the direction of where I'm staying. At a certain point, the autopilot came on, and I disappeared from the group, hopped in a cab, and headed back to the house.

It was in my best interest anyway to get back before everyone else. Overwhelmed with excitement after our arrival, Trav and I had neglected to pick bedrooms, and there was a good chance they were all occupied. I needed to nail down a plan for where I was going to sleep.

Everyone in the group seemed pretty reserved, but all it takes is one cowboy in an already-rowdy gang to start drawing forehead dicks or fire up the clippers and begin eliminating eyebrows.

I didn't want or need to be that specimen. I had down-played the weekend to my wife and certainly didn't want to stroll through the door Sunday afternoon with BONER writ-ten on my neck and a missing eyebrow.

With all the bedrooms accounted for, I took my infa-mous air mattress into a walk-in closet and inflated it. It filled up the closet, and I barricaded the sliding door with a spare dresser, hoping it would thwart any efforts to get to me.

The next day, I felt like a turd wrapped in hair and set on fire. One thing was apparent. I could no longer handle these types of weekends . . . or my liquor. I enjoyed the time away but should've eased up on the spirits. Catching a break from diaper duty and stepping on toys was wonderful, but life wasn't enjoyable with a hangover, and I missed my wife and daughter.

The drive home was misery. And knowing that I'd be back on duty as soon as I walked in the door with a hangover was going to be unbearable.

I definitely needed that time for me, but if I had a choice, next time it might be a hammock and a hotel room.

CHAPTER 10

It Took You Only Twelve Months

THE GRASS IS ALWAYS GREENER

I came home from the bachelor party refreshed and ready to tackle the shit out of parenthood with a renewed vigor. I was going to nail this motherfucker to the wall. I would adopt a substantial attitude change and look at this only as a "glass half full" situation. I would embrace the daily challenges and be the best dad I could be.

That lasted all of a week.

The Monday morning following a weekend of binge drinking came way too fast. We got up and pursued our daily routines. I got in the shower first and took Ava into the kitchen to fix breakfast while Jen hopped in the bathroom to apply her face. I slid back into my uniform—a T-shirt and bathing suit—and sat down to a breakfast of buttered toast and *Bubble Guppies*. I'm not sure I even realized that something was bothering me—I definitely didn't consciously know that there was trouble brewing beneath the surface . . . at least until Jen swaggered through the living room in high heels, all gussied up for work and smelling like some expensive Jo Malone perfume.

Whatever my internal conflict was, this had successfully gotten under my skin. Could it have been that I'd had a brief taste of the outside world and was jealous that Jen was jumping back into it while I stayed behind (yet again) to manage the life of a (almost) one-year-old? Whatever I was feeling, I did what guys do best: I internalized and buried it deep in my core, next to my secret affection for pedicures and Broadway musicals. I worked up a cookie-cutter smile and kissed her off into the exciting world of adult interaction and excitement.

That day and the few that followed, I made an honest effort to approach everything I was doing with this updated vim and revitalized vigor, but five minutes into whatever chore I was doing, it disappeared. I trudged about my business like the old cliché states, same shit different day. I assumed the position and let life take advantage of me without so much as paying for a nice date first.

Was I tired of playing house, bored with wiping down the counters, making dinner, and paying the utility bills? Was I fed up with having *zero* sick or vacation days or never getting a paycheck?

I could sense my old friend, depression, stopping by for another visit. Maybe it was the fact that Ava's first birthday was coming up, a significant milestone. It had me wondering how long I'd be a stay-at-home parent. I hadn't really thought about all of this until right now. Was there a chance for me to ever have anything more again?

While Jen was getting accolades at work, seeing ratings on her shows, getting raises and promotions and seeing her name in trade magazines, I had only an occasional stranger comment on my blog. Aside from that and my wife mentioning something in passing, no one was there to pat me on the back and say, "You're doing a great job, Adrian." I was without a cheering section. The stands were empty and the daily paper certainly wasn't paying me homage (LOCAL MAN CHANGES BLOWOUT USING ONLY TWO WIPES!) with any headlines of my own.

Maybe my frustration was a little bit of everything.

And then I felt like I came to a solid conclusion: I had built up resentment toward my wife.

There. I said it.

Inside my head, I was role-playing one-sided arguments, talking myself up as the victim. I was the poor, unsuspecting fish swimming along with his exciting little executive job, minding his own business, when *thwap!* I got foul-hooked and dragged up into the boat that was being a primary caretaker.

I managed to talk myself down through the course of the week and chose to not "pick this battle" with my wife. I was, however, resigned to the fact that my wife had it easier than me.

I had done a few loads of laundry that Thursday and had hung her shirts on the trim above the closet doorjamb. I took the ball all the way to the five-yard line, took a knee, and left the ball on the field as a test. I was curious to see if she would notice the work I'd done, pick up the ball and run it into the end zone herself—because, let's face it, this is a partnership, right? After she got home from work, we ate the Barefoot

Contessa dinner I'd spent two hours preparing, and soon after, she fell asleep on the sofa with Ava.

The next morning, she got ready for work and was about to head out when something in me just snapped. The ball remained in the red zone and Team Jen had taken what looked like a permanent time-out. The shirts hadn't moved.

I had taken great care in washing her garments properly, tumbling on low heat or laying flat when necessary. The least she could do was put the stuff away. Instead of asking her politely, I made a snarky comment. It was only a miniscule piece of what was bothering me, but it was the straw that broke the camel's back.

We proceeded to get into it, with me emphasizing that my job felt like it was twenty-four hours a day and that at least she was able to leave the office and catch a break after an eight- or ten-hour shift. Everything I did all day was for others and I barely ever had time to do anything for myself. I was not only responsible for Ava, but for maintaining the household (and the bills, laundry, cleaning, errands, etc., that go with it) as well.

I consistently tried to make life easier for her when she got home, and all I got were criticisms (mostly constructive, but I couldn't see them as such), which felt more like attacks on my parenting. I tried to compare us to other couples we knew, where the mom stayed home and the dad went to work—who took on what roles and did what around the house—but it just wasn't the same analogy.

Jen countered with the fact that she never got the option *or* choice to stay at home and that she felt forced to continue working, providing the bulk of our income. She wasn't working only to support our family, but was taking over the driver's seat at night and on the weekends because I needed some sort of break. She had always wanted to work, but her hope had been to find something she could do while taking care of the kids. The only way that would happen was if she didn't have to be the primary source of income. She, too, was resentful, not only of our situation, but also of me.

She was missing out on the day-to-day development of our daughter, watching as I posted pictures of Ava and me on Facebook, gallivanting around town having fun—bicycle rides along the beach, jogging together, playdates with other moms, feeding the ducks at the park, and spending a lot of time at the pool. She was jealous. She had struggled to find the energy to help around the house, being emotionally and physically exhausted from working sixty-plus hours a week, pumping breast milk in edit bays, while on conference calls, or during her commute, and being the mom Ava deserved once she got home. She was experiencing "working-mom guilt" and felt like she couldn't leave on the weekends for a pedicure or brunch with girlfriends because she couldn't bear the idea of leaving our daughter during any moment that she had free to spend with her. Even though she did a good job of hiding it, she was tired, sad and bitter.

She was late for work that morning and there was no kiss good-bye. Instead, the door slammed shut on the commotion we had created, and I sat in silence. We continued going back and forth via text message that morning.

Eventually we came to agree on one thing—that our situation was different. We were going against the ebb and flow of traditional working family models, and these feelings we were having were just a by-product of the role reversal. We faced a unique set of challenges moving forward.

I wanted her life and she wanted mine. But that wasn't realistic right now. We both agreed to open up the lines of communication and level the playing field with honesty and improved time management for the benefit of not only our relationship, but our family as a whole.

BACKSEAT DRIVER

After almost a year of riding around in my car, facing backward, staring into the same piece of leather over and over again, Ava finally lost it. In all fairness, I probably would've too. She staged daily protests, and it was time for an upgrade.

California State law mandates that a child be a year old or weigh twenty pounds in order to face forward in the car. Don't tell the CHP or child services, but for my driving sanity, I cheated it by two weeks.

Jen and I had already gone through the painful in-store research process several times before. It was agonizing walking up and down the car seat aisle, putting Ava in every demo, then watching my wife ask her how she liked it.

Front-runners were determined by whether or not she smiled or kicked her legs. She was eleven and a half months old. Did she really have an opinion?

We're putting all of our eggs in the basket of a girl who can barely talk? Each time, it ended the same way—with Jen and me polling a bunch of strange parents who walked by, inspiring an impromptu debate in the middle of the store with a bunch of random opinions and no final decision.

We continued our research online, evaluated the safety ratings, and found a winner. It was something without migraine-inducing fabric patterns and it was unisex, so we could pass it along to a sibling.

While Jen was at work one day, I decided to drive to Babies "R" Us (our favorite place) and take the plunge. Ava and I were on another adventure.

No matter what time of day, this place was always a circus. Unfortunately, they have everything we need. When I got to the cashier, she asked if I needed batteries with my purchase. I was dumbfounded. Was I a dumbass and had not researched this thing enough? Did I grab the vibrating version of the car seat accidentally?

A handful of tired and agitated pregnant women had gathered behind me in line. The pressure was on to fake like I knew what the hell I was talking about and win over their approval with nods.

Turned out, those cashiers are trained to ask everyone if they need batteries and I guessed right by saying no. The situation, however, deteriorated after it took me about six phone numbers to figure out which one our frequent shopper card was tied to. Oh well, can't win 'em all.

I pulled the car seat out in the parking lot and attempted to figure out how to install it. Didn't I just go through this a year ago? I was already educated on those pesky anchor points and hoped this experience wouldn't be nearly as intimidating.

This thing looked pretty sweet. Adjustable headrest, a recline function, extra padding, cubbyholes to hide cereal and a cup holder for those long drives when Ava likes to knock back a few cold ones.

She went bonkers being able to face forward for the first time, seeing everything that I was seeing. The excitement eventually subsided, but I realized that I now had a bigger problem on my hands.

Projectiles. If she wasn't happy with the music selection or sitting in traffic, now she was able to just chuck a bottle or a handful of Cheerios at me. The inside of my car became a war zone. Once a fresh, clean car, it was now covered in dried milk, crushed cereal powder, and toys.

Next time you're out for a drive and you see a car up ahead swerving in and out of its lane, wave hello. It's just me, steering with one hand and swatting at my kid in the back with the other, trying to locate a dropped sippy cup, baby, or sucker before she goes nuclear.

ONE NUTTY BIRTHDAY

It started with a knock at the door. I remember it vividly because the UPS driver banged on it like he was the DEA executing a search warrant, waking Ava up from her nap.

What can brown do for me?

TRY NOT TO BANG ON MY DOOR LIKE A CAVEMAN NEXT TIME YOU STOP BY WITH A PACKAGE.

When I opened up, the conversation went something like this:

UPS: UPS!

ME: Yeah, I can see that, man. You're wearing all brown and holding that package scanner. Wait a second. Marcus?

UPS: Yeah! Adrian? You're the same dude who lived here last year when I made all those baby deliveries.

ME: Yep, unfortunately that was me.

UPS: So what's up? You didn't have *another* kid, did you?

ME: No, dude. Don't even say that. Please. I don't even want that talk in the air. It might somehow happen.

UPS: I'm glad you're home today, man.

ME: Why is that? Normally, if I'm not here, you guys just dump it in front of my door or leave it in the leasing office.

UPS: Not today, my man.

I peeked into the hallway and saw two boxes the size of a refrigerator through a labyrinth of hallways in our complex. I wasn't expecting a package, especially nothing this size, and I was thinking this might be some sort of elaborate prank.

Once I got the boxes inside, I had no idea what to expect. Did someone mail themself to me? These boxes were gigantic, but surprisingly, didn't weigh that much.

I closed the door and ran to the closet like a kid on Christmas to get my Leatherman Multi-tool, a gift I've had for five years and used only three times. I gutted the box and there they were.

Seven hundred multicolored plastic balls. WTF was happening? Were we shooting *Double Dare* in my living room next week or what? I called my wife at work, wondering if this was one of her purchases that I wasn't privy to.

It was confirmed. They were for Ava's first birthday party. I never saw it coming.

Over the next few weeks, with so many repeat deliveries, Marcus and I were back to being bosom buddies. I was five minutes away from barbequing with this guy on the weekends.

Jen had bought a four-way acrylic tunnel, one hundred inflatable butterflies and beach balls, along with not one, but two specialized monogrammed outfits for the occasion. One outfit for before the cake and one for after.

She worked tirelessly to get custom swag bags ready for Ava's twenty friends. The monogrammed canvas bags included HABA wooden learning toys, tees, and designer Trumpette socks, and for the girls, more wooden toys, along with some great flower hats and headbands, and a bevy of other stuff.

Her friends weren't older than two. What in the hell was this? This party was going to be bigger than my twenty-first birthday. Admittedly, I spent my twenty-first drinking Prairie Fires and Jäger, throwing up in a trash bag, and being carried out of a country bar in my overalls, *but still*, this was getting out of hand.

We started to collect all the components of the big bash, which took up significant space. I was forced to build another pyramid in the dining room.

The swag bags were being assembled, a menu was being constructed, and our parents had booked their flights. We asked Jen's uncle, a renowned illustrator, to design a character of Ava, which we used for bag enclosures and direction cards. Bill gave us something that added a great personal touch.

The weekends leading up to the event took a stressful and chaotic tone, with a ton of last-minute shopping and planning. Our dining room began to remind me of an episode of *Hoarders*, but without the dead, flattened cat underneath all the gift bags. Stuff on top of stuff. It was perfect timing for our respective in-laws to come into town. We needed reinforcements.

It was a wild scene as my dad and father-in-law assisted me in grocery shopping. I made the decision to cook rather than have the party catered, which turned out to be one I would regret. We arranged to have the party on our apartment complex's community sundeck, which was about eighty yards from the kitchen.

On the morning of Ava's party, we put our relatives to work, having them truck items back and forth relentlessly for almost three hours. I was in crisis mode, running around the kitchen in my underwear, fashioning bruschetta and Israeli couscous salad, among other food fit to feed a hundred people.

Halfway through, I accidentally sliced my finger to the bone with one of our kitchen knives. I stopped (to make sure my finger wasn't on the floor), took a deep breath, and counted to ten. I snapped on some rubber gloves and pushed through it. I was too close to forfeiting this battle of *Iron Chef: Kid's Birthday Party*.

We expected guests by eleven a.m., the clown (sure, I said clown) by noon, and cake at one p.m. At ten forty-five a.m., I was still grinding, putting the finishing touches on several platters.

I flew around the kitchen like a wild man, carving ham and turkey, uncovering crudités, and folding napkins as Jen called from the sundeck to remind me that I had four minutes before the party started.

The food had finished being hauled down to the deck, and I needed those four minutes to get pretty. I gave myself a truck-stop rinse in the shower, clapped on some cologne, grabbed a collared shirt, and headed downstairs to greet everyone on the lawn leading up to the sundeck.

All of this hard work was about to pay off. Right? RIGHT!?

Our place was a disaster. Carrot skins and zucchini ends on the floor in the kitchen, wax soda bottles and Skittles spread across the dining room table from the three-tiered candy cake. Empty paper towel and aluminum foil tubes, pots, and pans sprawled everywhere. Opened luggage and clothes strewn throughout the premises.

We had taken it down to the wire.

I walked into the party and began the greeting frenzy. My energy levels were depleted, as I had been running around cooking for hours, so a Triscuit here, a black olive there, was all I had time for. I was shaking hands and kissing cheeks like I was running for mayor. It was as if I were being drawn and quartered, starting one conversation, then being torn to another, and finally heard my name being yelled from across the way to let the clown in. I wanted to dig my eyes out with baby spoons. Yes, the clown was here.

My wife had arranged for the clown to make an appearance. She was totally prepared. I brought her upstairs with her entourage. She asked me to join my wife and daughter in the center of the action. I agreed and played along with one of her "magical" tricks.

Evidently, the magic was me being punched in the face with a cream pie. Fun for everyone, right? I had just spent four solid minutes on a shower upstairs, along with ironing a linen (linen sucks to iron) shirt, and I was fuming inside. I forced a smile and wiggled my way through the guests I hadn't greeted yet, wiping the whipped cream in my eyes as I charged for the stairs.

I cleaned myself off, slammed a beer (we had beer at her party) to remove the edge, and returned to the deck. I was the first casualty of the day, but surely there would be others. If I came back, the clown certainly wouldn't target me again. I'm the host, for crying out loud. And, boy, was I wrong. The lady clown came right for me. This time, it was nondairy.

"HOW ABOUT A CRAYON PIRATE MUSTACHE?" she asked, as I squirmed left and right. She hit me with the goods. It was a blue Jack Sparrow special.

I did an about-face and headed back to the bathroom. Evidently, the crayon was "water-based" and I "shouldn't have any trouble getting it off." While my wife and the guests popped my daughter into the air on a multicolored parachute, I scrubbed vigorously at my chin in the guests' bathroom below the sundeck.

I returned to the festivities, this time, on guard. I slithered through the party under the radar, giving quiet low-fives and drawing the least amount of attention to myself as possible.

That's when I saw it. A live rabbit wearing sunglasses. Excitement moved to concern when the clown held him up, exposing his giant set of rabbit balls to the entire party. These hairy Easter eggs were suddenly the elephant in the room, as friends mimed WTFs to me from across the way.

I tried to divert the youngsters' attention over to another area to take the heat off of Balls Bunny. We had the polyester tunnel system, the inflatable ball pit, bouncy seats, a Rody, and padded mats with alphabet cutouts. It seemed to work, and the rabbit was put back inside the hat it came from.

I may paint a grim picture, but the clown was a great idea. She entertained the twenty children and certainly kept me on my toes. We said good-bye and moved on to the cake before kids started to drop like flies for naptime.

Ava doesn't eat a ton of sweets, and her eyes lit up as she watched the candle being lit on this giant sugar bomb of a cake. Watching the smile on her face made me realize that all of the running around and preparation was worth it.

I couldn't believe a year had passed so quickly. I made it. I was still alive.

But the sunshine daydream was quickly interrupted as a guest asked me for a few paper towels. Someone had spilled milk in the ball pit. Wonderful.

As our guests filed out of the party, I caught my breath and began the arduous task of cleaning up . . . the leftover Coronas! It was quiet as I sat there, wiping milk off of seven hundred individual plastic balls with baby wipes. I wondered if we had created a precedent that couldn't be beat. What happens when she turns two? The pony from the farmers market? Teenage Mutant Ninja Turtles on ice? Bieber?

So long as it doesn't involve any mammal testicles, it'll be fine by me.

CHAPTER 11

Thank You, Sir, May I Have Another?

BORN TO INSEMINATE

With the dust settled from Ava's first birthday party, life returned to normal. Jen and I had obviously talked before we got married about how many kids we wanted to have. I had always leaned toward three, maybe because that's how many kids were in my family. She had always leaned (and still does) toward four, probably for the same reason.

The reality is that we're not getting any younger. We had agreed on keeping our kids relatively close together in age, and so after Ava's odometer clicked past one, with breastfeeding in the rearview mirror and ovulation coming up ahead, the topic of another child began to come up in conversation. Repeatedly.

About a month after we found a reliable babysitter or two we could depend on from time to time, we made the decision to start "dating" again.

On one hand, I was excited about the possibility of going out to a dinner where I could actually cut, chew, and taste my food without having to cruise the restroom hallway burping and soothing. I was looking forward to a movie (in an actual theater!) where the love scene wasn't interrupted with violent shrieking.

I'd be lying if I said I wasn't looking forward to an occasional break for Jen and me to enjoy each other without distraction. In hindsight, we should've been making a bigger effort to do this all along.

On the other hand, I think Jen had a bad case of baby on the brain and was maybe using these dates to fulfill a secret agenda.

I was also finding incredible enjoyment in being Ava's daddy. She was just starting to really develop a personality, and I wasn't sure I wanted to split my attention with another baby just yet.

I also had to consider our situation a little differently this time. My wife was the one going to work every day, and I was the one taking care of Ava and maintaining the household. If this was the arrangement that we would continue to move forward with, I'd be responsible for not just one kid, but rather two kids under the age of two.

I was honest about my concerns, and her position was that we didn't even know if we could get pregnant again. Everything changes with time, and maybe it wouldn't be so easy the next time around. She expressed to me (again!) that it could take us weeks or months to get pregnant and that we were rolling the dice to either wait or go ahead with it. As much as her points seemed logical, I couldn't help but feel that she was using the Jedi mind trick on me. The Force was strong with this one.

We agreed to continue our date nights and not go out of our way to try to have another baby. Having said that, we also weren't going out of our way to *not* try to have another.

With any luck, I'd get a fair amount of "practice" with my lightsaber.

We officially had two date nights. The first was ravioli at the Italian place down the street, with two or three glasses of wine, followed by sex in our car (the babysitter was at the apartment!) surrounded by rattles and curdled sippy cups. The other was a matinee, and we'd failed to realize that it was a subtitled showing for the hearing impaired. We had to read the dialogue on the screen in giant yellow font as the action was happening. And if that weren't distracting enough, we had an earthquake halfway through the showing . . . while Ava was at home with the sitter. So far, our newfound courtship was textbook.

Two dates was all it took. Not weeks. Not months. Not years.

Yoda had won again, despite the raw power of my lightsaber. She came out of the bathroom one Saturday morning and showed me the stick. Perhaps she was incredibly fertile. Maybe I was just born to inseminate. Call the patent office. I smell a bumper sticker coming on.

Whatever the reason or circumstances, we were pregnant again.

We didn't expect this to happen so soon, but we were excited. How could we not be? It seemed like just yesterday we had gone through this whole process, and I was only now starting to feel comfortable with where we were.

We learned so many things in Ava's first year that it could only make our experience more grounded this next time around. I was now armed with knowledge and experience, even though that doesn't always mean everything. All kids are different and raising each child is always bound to have its own unique set of challenges.

What if it's another girl? Well, from a financial (cheapskate) standpoint, we can save a lot of money. We've already outfitted a girl through a year of life. There were already several bins of Ava's outgrown clothes and toys sitting next to my lonely LEGOs in storage. We could certainly recycle. Plus Ava would be thrilled to have a little sister to take care of and play dolls with; two best girlfriends . . . it had a nice ring to it.

And if it was a boy? From a selfish perspective, I would have a son. A son who would carry my last name into another generation. A son might be easier for me to relate to as he grows older. I might be better equipped to guide him through certain elements of life, social and beyond. He'd be only a little more than a year behind his sister, which means that he could still look out for her in school and kick ass if needed. And not that I've been thinking about it excessively, but he could also pick up some slack with the garbage, mowing the lawn, and raking the leaves, taking the dog out, wiping the baseboards, cleaning the toilets, getting the cars inspected, and sitting down with the accountant.

At the end of the day, it didn't really matter the gender of this baby. We were both just thankful to be able to give Ava a partner in crime.

THE BEST THING GOING

Believe it or not, any success I've experienced over this last year as a stay-at-home parent was due mostly to my ability to find the humor in everyday challenges. I had trouble in the beginning, and being a father didn't necessarily come naturally for me. I had to work at it. Not only did I learn a lot along the way about how to care for a baby, but I also learned a lot about myself. Hopefully, what we've done so far has created a good foundation and continues to work out for Ava and me as we both find our way through life.

It will be years before my daughter will be old enough to read about this journey we took together. But when the time comes, I want her to know . . .

This year of my life was a big pill to swallow.

From the moment your mom and I found out she was pregnant for the first time, we went through the anxiousness and concern about whether or not you were a boy or a girl, and more important, that you were healthy.

We had a great sense of relief when we found out that we were blessed enough to have a healthy daughter. We were so excited taking belly pictures of your mom every Sunday night and never missed a doctor's appointment, being there every step of the way. We shared in the joy of watching you grow before our very eyes on a computer screen. We passed around copies of the ultrasound to our parents and friends as we grew closer to meeting you.

Your mom dragged me to stores almost every weekend (I missed some big games!) to buy you clothes and soft blankets. A few weeks before you came into this world, we decorated your nursery together without killing each other. I held Mommy's hand in the operating room during your delivery, and hearing you cry for the first time nearly brought me to my knees. There was nothing more powerful than knowing that I had helped create you.

Because of you, our lives have been forever transformed.

I will forever cherish holding you for the first time, enjoying your smell. Rocking you to sleep on my chest, giving you your first bottle, and changing your first diaper.

We spent almost every day together, going for walks on the beach, grocery shopping, and running errands. You occasionally puked in my hair and you ruined most of my shirts.

I took pride in watching you discover and explore your ears, mouth, fingers, and toes. Your facial expressions and laughter were priceless . . . as was watching your personality expand and develop, seeing you roll, crawl, and walk for the very first time.

You taught me about love, patience, and devotion. You

gave me purpose during a time when I wasn't sure what mine was.

This last year has been filled with so many ups and downs. I lost my job during the height of a recession. I experienced a bout of depression, low self-esteem, and a lack of confidence.

Staying at home and raising you over the past year has helped me discover more about myself and what I'm capable of. Without even knowing it, you were responsible for rebuilding those traits within me. You were the impetus for me writing this book.

I let go of a career as a successful executive in a field I loved and embraced a nontraditional reversal of gender roles as a stay-at-home dad. I also managed to turn these experiences of being a dad into a new career for myself.

I paid bills, dusted, swept, and mopped. I did laundry, bought flowers, took care of the dog, and cooked dinner from scratch almost every night. I drove to the pediatrician, sang songs in the car, became a regular at the playground, and played dress-up with you because it made you smile.

I taught you about manners and sharing, how to sit on the potty and showed you the difference between right and wrong. I peeked in on you sleeping and fixed your covers late at night. I put Band-Aids on your boo-boos and held you tight when you were scared of the thunder.

It took me a minute to come around, but *this* is my dream job and I consider myself extremely lucky to have it. I wouldn't trade it for anything in the world.

Am I worried about what people think of me?

I shouldn't be. I'm doing one of the most important jobs there is.

I don't need to be the breadwinner to know that I'm leaving my mark.

While I lost a job, I gained a lot more. I gained perspective. I gained a best friend.

My daughter.

I love you, Ava.

After 365 days, only one big question remains. How in the fuck am I going to do this again with two of them?

ACKNOWLEDGMENTS

For their love, friendship and tireless support of this endeavor: Jen, Ava and Charlie, Mom, Dad, Eric and Travis, Shirley Kulp, Bob and Elaine Mayer, the Kulp, Mayer, Hellwig, and Trost families.

For their endless patience, advice, direction and shared vision, I'd like to thank Mark Krick, Jeff Baldinger, Sheila McDermott, Erin Malone, Doug Robinson, Danielle Perez and her colleagues at New American Library/Penguin Group.

Photo by Jen Mayer Kulp 2012

Adrian Kulp has worked as a comedy booking agent for CBS late-night television, as an executive for Adam Sandler's Happy Madison Productions, and as a vice president of development for Chelsea Handler's Borderline Amazing Productions. He now lives in Rockville, Maryland, with his wife, Jennifer, and their two kids, Ava and Charlie.

CONNECT ONLINE

WWW.DADORALIVE.COM

FACEBOOK.COM/DADORALIVE

TWITTER.COM/DAD_OR_ALIVE